THE NEWS MEDIA

WHAT EVERYONE NEEDS TO KNOW®

THE NEWS MEDIA

WHAT EVERYONE NEEDS TO KNOW®

C. W. ANDERSON,
LEONARD DOWNIE JR.,
MICHAEL SCHUDSON

OXFORD
UNIVERSITY PRESS

Oxford University Press is a department of the University of Oxford.
It furthers the University's objective of excellence in research, scholarship,
and education by publishing worldwide. Oxford is a registered
trade mark of Oxford University Press in
the UK and certain other countries.

"What Everyone Needs to Know" is a registered trademark of
Oxford University Press.

Published in the United States of America by Oxford University Press
198 Madison Avenue, New York, NY 10016, United States of America.

Library of Congress Cataloging-in-Publication Data
Names: Anderson, C. W. (Christopher William), 1977– author. |
Downie, Leonard, author. | Schudson, Michael, author.
Title: The news media : what everyone needs to know /
C.W. Anderson, Leonard Downie Jr., and Michael Schudson.
Description: New York : Oxford University Press, 2016. |
Series: What everyone needs to know
Identifiers: LCCN 2016006485 (print) | LCCN 2016008843 (ebook) |
ISBN 9780190206192 (hardcover : alk. paper) |
ISBN 9780190206208 (pbk. : alk. paper) | ISBN 9780190206215 (Updf) |
ISBN 9780190206222 (Epub)
Subjects: LCSH: Journalism—United States—History. |
Journalism—Objectivity.
Classification: LCC PN4855 .A63 2016 (print) | LCC PN4855 (ebook) |
DDC 071/.309—dc23
LC record available at http://lccn.loc.gov/2016006485

1 3 5 7 9 8 6 4 2
Paperback printed by R.R. Donnelley, United States of America
Hardback printed by Bridgeport National Bindery, Inc.,
United States of America

CONTENTS

2 The Present 60

3 The Future 120

THE NEWS MEDIA

WHAT EVERYONE NEEDS TO KNOW®

INTRODUCTION

It might seem presumptuous to write a book promising readers "what everyone needs to know about the news media" in the year 2016. After all, it seems to many outside observers that the last two decades have transformed the news from something solid and understandable to something amorphous, uncertain, and "postindustrial."[1] Journalism and "the news" used to be what journalists said it was, the story goes. It was created for recognizable news organizations with money generated by long-standing business models using traditional newsroom workflows. In the twenty-first century, on the other hand, everything seems up for grabs—how journalism gets produced, how it gets funded, what its public purpose is, and even what *it* is.

It is the contention of this book that, popular claims of indecipherability notwithstanding, there actually is a lot we know about the news media, and journalism. We know a great deal about journalism's past, for starters, and we know far more than we ever did before. The academic field of "journalism history" has grown by leaps and bounds in the past several decades and is now replete with its own specialty journals, conferences, and historical symposia. As the field of journalism history has grown, we have also learned that many of the profession's cherished myths, if not always entirely inaccurate,

1. Anderson, Bell, and Shirky (2013). *Post Industrial Journalism: Adapting to the Present*.

are far more complicated than they appear at first blush. This is not to say that journalism historians agree on everything, of course; like good academics, they constantly argue about a great many things related to the history of news. Nevertheless, it is one of the goals of this book to make leading historical scholarship available for and understandable by everyday curious readers.

We also, believe it or not, know a great deal about journalism *today*—and as a society we probably know more than seems immediately apparent. It is easy to look at newspaper companies teetering on the edge of insolvency, rapidly changing digital formats, and strategy memos from insurgent news organizations, and conclude that everything is unknowable and uncertain. But digital news, at this point, has been in existence for more than two decades and there has been a great deal of data and hard-earned wisdom accumulated along the way. There is more actual *data* available on news than ever before—just to name one example, the Pew "State of the News Media" reports have only been published since 2001 but have come out annually since then. And there is now a cluster of quasi-academic think tanks, ranging from the Reuters Institute at Oxford to the Tow Center at Columbia, producing a seemingly endless supply of reports for general, professional, and academic audiences that did not exist a decade ago. Beyond just data, however, there is a great deal of accumulated *wisdom* about journalism today. News industry professionals have actually learned a lot about their business in the past few years, and we hope to share some of that accumulated wisdom with you in the pages that follow.

We admit that we (along with everyone else) are on far shakier ground when it comes to the *future* of news, although there is perhaps no shame in this, given that future-prediction is usually the provenance of prophets and fortunetellers, not scholars. Even over the course of the writing of this book the authors saw new developments—such as the increased journalistic power of digital platforms like Facebook, or the massive leak of documents that became known as the Panama Papers and the unprecedented journalistic collaboration that helped publish them—become pressing issues in ways that we did not expect when we started our work. This should be a warning not to put too much trust in prognostication, no matter what the source. However, it would be a disservice to our curious readers to leave discussions of what we might reasonably expect to happen in journalism out of the conversation housed in these pages. And it is here that knowing a bit about the past and the present becomes useful. While it is impossible to know for certain what the years ahead will bring, a familiarity with both the history of news and the ways it currently works give us far more leverage to speculate about what *might* happen ten or even twenty years from now. And even if these speculations turn out to be entirely off base, we hope that the answers to some of the questions here about the future will spark good conversation at the very least!

Given all this, it will not come as a surprise that the book is divided into three chapters: "The Past," "The Present," and "The Future" of news. In the initial drafting stages, Michael Schudson took on the past, Leonard Downie the present, and C.W. Anderson crossed his fingers and tackled the future. However, over the process of writing, the authorial divisions between these sections blurred, and we are convinced that the final product stands as much as a unified distillation of our thought process as it would be reasonable to hope for.

We expect that different sets of readers will initially approach this book with different objectives in mind. General students may find a great deal of value in the discussion of journalism's past. Working reporters and journalism students, in particular, may come to this book most interested in chapter 2, "The Present." And who doesn't love a bit of future-of-news prognostication? But it is also our hope that readers who come for specific reasons will decide to stick around and learn things about the news that they did not initially expect. We hope busy news executives can learn about the history of their profession. We hope that journalism historians can get quickly up to date on the most informed speculation about what the twenty-first century might bring for the field. And most importantly, perhaps, we hope that all readers will walk away from this book with a sense that, although there is much we still do not know about journalism, there is much else that we do.

1

THE PAST

When and where was the world's first newspaper published?

This depends on what we mean by "newspaper." Suppose we mean something that is *published*—that is, intended to be circulated to multiple persons, many of whom may be unknown to the publisher (unlike a personal letter); *periodical* (unlike a broadside published to communicate news about a specific occasion without any promise or expectation of further publication); *printed* (thereby making possible a general circulation much more difficult and expensive to achieve in handwritten form); and *present-centered* in its subject matter. Then we can pinpoint an answer fairly well: The first newspaper was produced in Strasbourg, Germany, by a printer, Johann Carolus, in 1605. Others would follow soon thereafter.

The first newspaper in English was not far behind. It was published in 1620. What may surprise the modern reader is that it was published not in London or Oxford but in Amsterdam, which was also the home of the first newspaper in French. Both French- and English-language newspapers in Amsterdam translated German and Dutch newspapers for the French and English markets.

And the first American newspaper?

The first American newspaper, that is, the first newspaper in the English colonies in North America, in what was to become the United States, was published in Boston in 1690, *Publick Occurences Both Foreign and Domestick*. Its proprietor, Benjamin Harris, promised in it to furnish readers monthly—more often only if "any Glut of Occurrences happen," with a faithful account of "such considerable things as have arrived unto our Notice." The news covered would be that of "Memorable Occurents of Divine Providence" and "Circumstances of Publique Affairs." Note the passivity of publishing only things that "have arrived unto our Notice," the intention of normally publishing only once a month, and the assumption that the newsworthy actors to cover were both divine and human.

It was the human actors who tripped up these ambitions, principally Harris himself. He had failed to secure the royal governor's permission to publish, and his paper was shut down after its first issue, never to reappear. The next venture into journalism would not emerge for more than a decade—also in Boston, the *Boston Newsletter*, in 1704. It was conceived by John Campbell, Boston's postmaster, a bookseller, and—unusually for early newspaper entrepreneurs—*not* himself a printer. Like other early papers in the colonies that would follow, the content was primarily news items reprinted from London newspapers.

And there was no such thing as journalism until the 1600s?

There was no such thing as a newspaper—published, periodical, printed, present-centered. There was no such thing as journalism—an arena of human activities differentiated from others, with its own definition; a social domain that people might understand themselves to be vocationally or avocationally a part of; a set of ideas and practices at least partially distinct from other fields.

This does not mean there was no such thing as news, the gathering of news, and the dissemination of news. Whenever language developed, surely there were people who shouted to others in their group something like, "Run! A predator!"

Surely there were some ancient ancestors of Captain Ahab who called out to their crew, "Whale on the starboard bow!" And no doubt after writing developed, people passed notes to one another with news like "Enemy troops sighted just over the mountain" or "Amy loves Brian." These are all items of relevant information about the present. But that is a long way from journalism as a distinguishable social function and specialized pursuit.

Before there were newspapers, sermons sometimes had news-like purposes. Sermons were periodical, published for a known community but one that might at any Sunday include also some strangers. Sermons might even be printed later, in book form, although by then their value as news of current affairs would have expired. We know that more than a few sermons in England in the late 1500s and early 1600s shared with parishioners information about the outcome of military battles abroad, putting them in the context of God's intentions. But sermons, even when they provided some world news, were delivered for religious purposes in a distinctively religious setting. Important church-sponsored newspapers notwithstanding, the lineage of the newspapers that for four hundred years would be the heart of journalism goes back to states, parties, and commerce, not churches.

There were scattered impulses toward organized provision of news as public communication, at least as far back as ancient Rome, but they left no legacy for what would become journalism as we have known it since the 1600s. In China, a court gazette had been published for a thousand years before Peking Gazette was established early in the eighteenth century, but its audience was court officials, not a general public. The first recognizably modern newspapers in China began in the nineteenth century under the initiative of Protestant missionaries.

The recency of newspapers and of journalism should not seem odd. Storytelling is old but novels in the West appear as a narrative form in the 1700s. Humans have presumably always been curious and inquiring but organized science begins as a distinctive vocation, field, and pursuit in the 1600s. People have likewise always had interest in novel developments around them, but a field centered on regularly disseminating notice of and commentary about these topical events (or some subset of them) has been organized as an intentional pursuit for only about four hundred years.

What were early newspapers like? Who started them and why?

The early newspapers—those of the 1600s and roughly the first half of the 1700s—were all, as our definition of "newspaper" suggests, published for a general audience, printed, periodical, and for the most part present-minded in content. Still, there was no single model of what a newspaper should be, but a set of models, and many blended versions of them.

As historian Charles Clark has suggested, writing of Britain and its colonies, the eighteenth century witnessed four models emerge. One prominent model was the official state-issued news vehicle coming into use in the 1600s. In England, the *London Gazette* began as a government publication in 1665. It was a collection of official state announcements. Another model was the "advertiser." In some cases, advertisers contained nothing *except* advertisements. These might be distributed without charge to booksellers, coffeehouses, and inns. London's *City Mercury* began this way in the 1670s. By the 1690s, it contained also business news, not advertisements only.

A third form was the propaganda journal or a publication guided by a strong political position. Finally, there were literary and satirical journals and magazines. England's most celebrated example was *The Spectator*, begun in 1710 by Joseph Addison—a lively, humorous, and sometimes philosophically inclined writer. Remarkably for a time in which newspapers typically published once a week, Addison managed for several years to produce his blog-like first person publication daily. The number of newspapers in its various forms grew over the 1700s; London counted twenty-three newspapers by 1790.

And early newspapers in the American colonies?

There were very few of them. The first to be sustained beyond one issue was the *Boston Newsletter* begun in 1704. When Benjamin Franklin's older brother James considered starting a newspaper in Boston more than a decade later, friends tried to discourage him on the grounds that one newspaper was plenty for Massachusetts. James went ahead nonetheless, issuing the *New England Courant* and providing young Ben, hired as his apprentice, his first experience in the printer's trade.

In all of the thirteen American colonies in 1760 there were about twenty newspapers, doubling to forty by 1775, located primarily in the population centers of Boston, New York, Baltimore, and Philadelphia. They were four-page weekly publications generally organized like the London journals before them in two or three columns on a page. Their contents: an assortment of local advertising, some paragraphs of local gossip, and large amounts of European political and economic intelligence reprinted directly from London newspapers (and the London papers often reprinted from Dutch newspapers that translated Dutch and German and Italian accounts). When Thomas Jefferson was Secretary of State under President George Washington, he worked with editors who were willing to print articles from the *Gazette de Leyte*, a Dutch newspaper much more sympathetic to the French Revolution than the London papers from which most American printers routinely took their news. Jefferson understood very well that reprinting, or what today is called aggregating, was how American newspapers worked.

In any given colonial newspaper, political news of other American colonies rarely appeared. Local political news was rarely noted or discussed. Printers typically did not see their newspapers as either political instruments or professional agencies for gathering news. They just printed what came to them. They avoided controversy although, by generally printing whatever individuals might voluntarily send them for publication, they were not always able to escape it. The preponderance of foreign news, however, was overwhelming. When Ben Franklin moved to Philadelphia and started his own newspaper there, the *Pennsylvania Gazette*, only some 6% of news items over its several decades touched on politics in Philadelphia or in the colony of Pennsylvania.

There was little sense that the general public was an appropriate audience for political information. When the occasional pamphlet took up a political matter, it was written with the colonial assembly or legislature as audience, not the public at large. Not until the 1740s did some writers produce pamphlets that explicitly focused on the general citizenry as readers. This was particularly the case in New York, Philadelphia, and Boston as political conflict became more common in these centers of commerce and commotion.

What does the First Amendment mean?

The First Amendment is just one sentence: "Congress shall make no law respecting an establishment of religion, or prohibiting the free exercise thereof; or abridging the freedom of speech, or of the press; or the right of the people peaceably to assemble, and to petition the government for a redress of grievances." If we focus just on the part of that sentence concerning the news media, it is: "Congress shall make no law . . . abridging the freedom of speech, or of the press." What could be simpler? But it turns out to be complicated enough to have spawned thousands of books and law journal articles. And although one Supreme Court justice (Justice Hugo Black) declared that "'No law' means no law," that was wishful thinking on his part. A lot of laws and a lot of judicial interpretation have tried to pinpoint what limits of speech and press might be acceptable under the terms of the First Amendment.

The First Amendment meant one thing to the men who penned it and those who approved it as an amendment to the United States Constitution in 1791. It has come to mean something very different over time. It did not come to be the cornerstone of the law of the press until the twentieth century.

And what exactly did it mean to those who wrote it and made it part of the Constitution? Historians do not speak on this question with a single voice, but most agree that, despite some differences in emphasis among the founders, the most important word in the free-press clause of the First Amendment—"Congress shall make no law . . . abridging freedom of speech or of the press" is the first word: "Congress." In fact, James Madison had proposed an amendment in which the states, as well as the federal government, would have been prohibited from interfering with freedom of the press, but that amendment was defeated. What remained was a prohibition of federal laws abridging freedom of the press, not state laws. As Thomas Jefferson explained to Abigail Adams in 1804: "While we deny that Congress have a right to control the freedom of the press, we have ever asserted the right of the States, and their exclusive right, to do so." More than once, when Jefferson was President (1801–1809), he encouraged political allies to sue the press for libel if they were criticized in the newspapers—so long as they sued in state courts.

It would be more than a century before the modern First Amendment began to take shape. It was not until 1925 (in the case of *Gitlow v. New York*) that the Supreme Court announced that the First Amendment applied to the states, not just the federal government. It was not until 1931 that the Supreme Court first overturned a state law restricting free speech or press for violating the First Amendment.

Beginning in the 1920s and growing more secure since the famous 1964 case of *New York Times v. Sullivan*, a Supreme Court view emerged that the First Amendment permits a distinction between "high" value and "low" (or at least "lower") value speech. Speech about elections, politics, and public policy, including speech critical of government or of government officials, is high value speech. This is the kind of speech that was most on the minds of the founders. Supreme

Court decisions have determined that it is very important to protect political speech but that some kinds of speech are clearly unprotected—demonstrably false advertising, libelous speech or defamation, speech enacting a criminal conspiracy, or "fighting words" that are intended to cause and may have the effect of causing violence.

The speech at issue in the Sullivan case was an advertisement in the *New York Times* designed to raise funds to defend Martin Luther King, Jr. against a lawsuit in Alabama. L. B. Sullivan, the Montgomery, Alabama public safety commissioner, although not named in the advertisement, was the public official who oversaw Montgomery's police force, which was criticized in the ad. Sullivan sued the *Times* for publishing defamatory statements. The US Supreme Court unanimously found in favor of the *Times*. Its decision certified that libel suits against news organizations by public officials would be very, very difficult to win. The public official would have to show not only that the news organization published false and damaging statements but also that it did so knowingly and with "malice."

The distinction between high value speech and other speech, as well as other distinctions and doctrines that shape First Amendment law, have arisen in twentieth-century judicial decisions. They were unknown to the founders. So the First Amendment has varied across US history. What has become invariant is the pride the US press takes in the fact that journalists are the only occupational group to be mentioned in the US Constitution ("...or of the press"). What is also clear is that US judicial doctrine about freedom of the press, for all of its variations, is less likely to approve government regulation of or limitations on wide-open free speech and free press than any other contemporary democratic country, even countries with substantial and seriously defended liberty of the press.

How is the US tradition of the free press different from traditions in other democracies?

Most democracies enforce "right of reply" statues where news organizations that have published critical remarks about, say, a candidate for office must, upon request, provide a forum for the offended individual to respond. The US Supreme Court declared that such laws violate the First Amendment. Many European democracies prohibit "hate speech" by law. US law does not. European legal thinkers defend their version of free speech and press as ultimately serving democracy better than the First Amendment. A "right of reply" law requires private news organizations to give someone they have criticized or attacked a voice, but it does not limit the organization from saying what it wishes. Isn't this government enforcement of "more speech" better than the "less speech" that would result without it?

And hate speech has a chilling effect on members of disparaged—indeed, hated—minority groups. Hate speech intimidates, and it may also incite or encourage violence. Does outlawing hate speech then not serve a central democratic value, so central that government should be willing to enact carefully drafted hate speech laws? Some American legal thinkers agree with European thinkers in defending bans on hate speech, but others see danger in any prohibitions on putatively political speech.

However distinctive the First Amendment, after World War II a faith in free speech and press became widely professed in many parts of the world, if incompletely established. The Universal Declaration of Human Rights, endorsed by the United Nations in 1948, includes Article 19 which declares, in its entirety, "Everyone has the right to freedom of opinion and expression; this right includes freedom to hold opinions without interference and to seek, receive and impart information and ideas through any media and regardless of frontiers."

How could the American founding fathers have approved the First Amendment and also supported federal subsidies for newspapers and also passed the Sedition Act of 1798 that made criticizing the federal government a crime?

Try to see it their way: contemporary understandings of the First Amendment would not have made much sense to the founders. They certainly did not see the First Amendment as forbidding the federal government from *encouraging* the press. It only prohibits the government from *abridging* press freedom. So in 1792, the year after the First Amendment became law, the Congress approved and President Washington signed into law the Postal Act. In setting up the ground rules for the postal system, the Act provided that newspapers circulated through the mail—as newspapers typically were distributed—would qualify for a reduced postal rate. When newspapers were mailed to other newspapers, they could be mailed entirely free of charge. This was anything but trivial to early editors. Newspapers of the day were "aggregators." They got their content by reprinting stories found in other newspapers for their own local readers. So the Postal Act was, in a sense, a direct government subsidy of the primary means of news-gathering for the early American press; the newspapers could scarcely have survived without a ready and cheap supply of "exchange" newspapers.

The Sedition Act (1798) was something else again. By any plausible reading, it abridged freedom of the press. It authorized fines or imprisonment for editors who printed "any false, scandalous and malicious writing . . . against the government of the United States." But it became law at the time of an undeclared war with France in an era when government was understood to be a vulnerable institution. Government was not a towering force issuing edicts from marble halls, defended by an extensive network of military fortresses, supported by highways it built and taxes it collected. The founders truly believed that calling into question the government or its individual officeholders genuinely threatened the survival of an untested republican government not yet a decade old.

In fact, about a quarter of all the "Republican" newspapers—those unsympathetic to the John Adams administration and its "Federalist" orientation—were charged under the Sedition Act and some of the editors went to prison. That did not, however, prevent the champion of the Republican opposition, Thomas Jefferson, from being elected president in 1800. The Sedition Act expired in 1801 and nothing like it would be renewed until World War I.

How did the founders reconcile the Sedition Act with the First Amendment? They didn't. The Act passed narrowly. Madison and Jefferson strongly opposed it. But the courts did not weigh in. At that time, there was not yet a tradition of judicial review to authorize the Supreme Court to decide if an act of Congress was a violation of the Constitution and therefore void. That would not begin until 1803 in the case of *Marbury v. Madison*.

Why were European visitors to the United States in the nineteenth century so often astonished—and sometimes appalled—by the American press?

The astonishment was clear—there were just so *many* newspapers! And they could be found not only in urban areas far from political capitals but even in very small towns. Why so many? A large part of the answer is that the American founders acted to encourage the establishment of papers. The federal government established post offices throughout the country. By 1830 the US had four times as many post offices per 100,000 people as Britain, fifteen times as many as France. The government also subsidized newspaper circulation by providing discounted postal rates to newspapers and free circulation in the mails for newspapers mailed to other newspapers. The latter was a significant boost for newsgathering since papers freely reprinted news items from other papers to make up a large proportion of their content.

Another factor in the establishment of newspapers was the sense people had that the newspaper was an emblem of a community, not so much a newsgatherer as a chamber of commerce that advertised the glories of its city or town to others beyond it. In the mid-nineteenth century, as the frontier was pushed westward and as new communities of small populations and limited economic resources sought to grow by attracting new settlers, the towns promoted the establishment of colleges, "grand hotels," and newspapers to boost their economic prospects.

What was appalling to visitors was the arrogance, vitriol, and hyperbole of the partisan papers of the nineteenth century. The most famous of the European admirers of American newspapers was the young French civil servant and public intellectual, Alexis de Tocqueville. He visited in 1830–1831, and wrote glowingly of newspapers, "We should underrate their importance if we thought they just guaranteed liberty; they maintain civilization." At the same time, he complained of the violence and vulgarity of the language of American newspapers. In fact, he found it a saving grace that the newspapers were dispersed around the country rather than concentrated in a capital city—this way they could do less harm. It was for him a virtue of the press that it "makes political life circulate in every corner" but the power of the press nonetheless worried him. Individually, he thought, the newspapers were powerless but collectively the press was "the first of powers" after the people themselves.

How did newspapers become mass market media?

This was not an inevitable development and it did not happen everywhere. It happened in Japan; it happened in the Nordic countries, Britain, and Germany; but newspaper reading remained much less widespread in France, Italy, Greece, Spain, and Portugal. In 2000, there were more than 500 newspapers sold per 1,000 adults in Norway, Finland, and Sweden, more than 250 in the United States, the Netherlands, Germany, and Britain, but less than 200 in France, Spain, and Italy, less than 100 in Portugal and Greece.

The market for newspapers grew enormously in India but only from the 1970s on. Until then, the most prominent Indian newspapers were in English, the language of only a small proportion—about 5%—of the population. The mass marketing of newspapers took off in India for multiple reasons, technological change among them: not until computerization was it possible to easily print in India's many languages and many scripts.

In the United States, there were two key moments in making newspapers mass market commodities. First, the "penny press" developed in the 1830s and 1840s in the major Atlantic seaboard cities of Boston, New York, Philadelphia, and Baltimore. The penny papers were cheap, sold on the street daily by newsboys rather than being sold only by subscription through the mail, and the leading penny papers emphasized local news, including coverage of crime and the courts. The proprietors of the penny papers avowed their commercial ambitions and hoped that high circulation and the advertising it would attract would make them successful enterprises. This proved to be a very effective business model up until the digital age.

The second stage came in the last decades of the nineteenth century when several news entrepreneurs found ways to cut costs or draw in new readers or both. Joseph Pulitzer's pioneering leadership of the *New York World* in the 1880s and 1890s provided larger headlines, more illustrations, more lively news coverage, and more attention to topics of general interest (like sports) and topics that would draw in nontraditional newspaper readers, notably women and immigrants. In Detroit, Cleveland, Cincinnati, St. Louis, and Buffalo, publisher James Scripps cut the size of the newspaper page, reducing the cost of newsprint, and cut the investment in news relayed by telegraph to reduce reporting costs. Scripps held that lavish expenditures on reporting were "not appreciated by the common people whom we should seek for our constituency." His formula for reaching people of modest means proved very successful and was widely copied; the number of US daily newspapers rose rapidly from not quite six hundred in 1870 to 2600 by 1910, the high water mark for US newspapers, never again equaled.

Did Karl Marx write regularly for Horace Greeley's New York Tribune?

Yes, he did. He contributed 350 columns between 1853 and 1861 and he coauthored another dozen with his comrade Friedrich Engels (who solo-authored 125 himself). This all began when *Tribune* editor Charles Dana was traveling in Germany in 1848 and met Marx in Cologne. He must have been impressed with Marx, who was already well known for the pamphlet he and Engels had just published, *The Communist Manifesto*. Several years later, Dana invited Marx to write about the impact of the revolutions of 1848 in Europe on Germany and this would lead to the sustained relationship with the *Tribune*. Marx ended his relationship with the *Tribune* a decade later when Dana left the paper; the paper became less staunchly abolitionist, and the American Civil War left American readers less interested in European affairs than before.

A century later, President Kennedy would speak to the American Newspaper Publishers Association, reminding them that an American publisher had once employed Karl Marx, communism's founding father. Marx complained frequently about the low salary the *Tribune* paid and Kennedy suggested, in jest, that if the stingy publisher of the *Tribune* had only paid Marx better, a great deal of unpleasantness with communism might have been avoided.

The vast majority of Marx's columns concern European political affairs. They are Marx's own observations, none of them based on discussions or interviews with sources in positions of power (or any other sources). That was the normal journalism of the day.

Why did Abraham Lincoln spend so many hours in the telegraph office during the Civil War?

The electronic telegraph was invented in 1844 and newspapers quickly made good use of it. The United States government, however, did not. When the Civil War began in 1861, government officials who wanted to send a telegram went to a commercial telegraph office and stood in line like everybody else.

In May 1862, a year after the war broke out, the War Department, next door to the White House, opened its own telegraph office. Before then, Lincoln sent about one telegram a month. Historian Tom Wheeler writes that on May 24, 1862 Lincoln had his "online breakout" and sent nine telegrams in a single day. He got into the habit of walking over to the telegraph office several times a day and reading whatever telegrams had come in. During major battles he even slept in the telegraph office. Even as a young man, Lincoln had been an enthusiast for new inventions and new technology. With the nation's very existence at stake during the war, Lincoln wanted to be as close to the front lines as he could—he wanted the news as quickly as possible and he wanted his unruly generals in the field to know that he was watching them closely.

Other presidents later would also show interest in new media technologies. This included Franklin D. Roosevelt, who was an early pioneer of radio, sensing quickly what that medium offered for someone who spoke with warmth, humor, and a winning sincerity. Radio proved a great way to communicate directly and intimately with Americans. Barack Obama famously has used a BlackBerry mobile phone.

When was the first interview? And how did interviewing become a standard practice in newsgathering?

Interviews did not become part of journalism until the nineteenth century and then in the United States before anywhere else. The first interview may have been James Gordon Bennett's in New York for the *New York Herald*—the penny paper he owned, edited, and wrote for—as he played both police detective and reporter in covering the sensational murder of Helen Jewett in 1836. Or it may have been Horace Greeley's interview with the Mormon leader Brigham Young in 1859, printed in his *New York Tribune* in a question-and-answer format. This was so unusual at the time that Greeley prefaced it with an explanation of what this format meant: "Such is, as nearly as I can recall, the substance of nearly two hours of conversation, wherein much was said incidentally that would not be worth reporting, even if I could remember and reproduce it." It seems clear that Joseph McCullagh was the first reporter to interview a US president for publication: Andrew Johnson, in 1867.

Interviewing spread quickly in the United States. Thompson Cooper, writing for the *New York World* in 1871, was the first reporter ever, from any country, to interview the Pope. Boasting of the event, as newspapers and later other news media to this day would continue to brag about exclusive interviews, the *World* crowed, "The Roman Catholic Church is the oldest, as the interview is almost the youngest, of the institutions of mankind. And they are this morning presented face to face. . . . The Church and the Press have kissed each other." American reporters would be the first to interview British Cabinet officers and European heads of state and monarchs in the following decades.

British journalists were faster than other Europeans to adopt interviewing but they recognized that the Americans got there first—"The interview," wrote British journalist William Stead in 1902, "was a distinctively American invention." For a long time, interviewing was regarded as undignified. One veteran American reporter recalled in the late nineteenth century how, in the good old days, Washington correspondents were "neither eavesdroppers nor interviewers, but gentlemen, who had a recognized position in society, which they never abused." (This, of course, is nonsense.) He judged interviewing a "pernicious habit" and "a dangerous method of communication between our public men and the people."

Why was interviewing judged to be pernicious? Well, it was just plain unseemly. Louisville, Kentucky, editor Henry Watterson complained of interviewers who undertook "the hold-up in the (railroad) station" and the "ambuscade in the lobby of the hotel"—thereby providing "an added terror to modern travel." And it was so impertinent! "Public men," as the phrase of the day had it, were normally of high status and social pedigree. Journalists were typically far from it. Anyone could become a journalist. But the relative classlessness of America—compared to Europe—made resistance to the interview more feeble in the United States than in the Old World.

In time, interviewing became standard practice for practically all American journalists and for more and more journalists abroad. Very likely its ready acceptance in the United States has to do with the relative egalitarianism of American public life, the relative absence of strongly marked class divisions. Decades later, chewing gum, the Hershey bar, and later still McDonald's and Starbucks would be US agents of informality in other parts of the world, but interviewing was an early American export in the same informalizing direction.

For European critics of interviewing, journalism was a calling to be practiced by people with high literary ambitions. The model form of the newspaper article was an essay—it was normally an analysis of (rather than a report of) current political and economic events. It was more likely to be undertaken from a private study than from a newsroom. Journalists aspired to literary flair and analytical acumen. Interviewing, in contrast, ironed out these high-minded intellectual and literary aspirations as if they were so many wrinkles in a shirt.

What were immigrants reading as they flocked to the United States in the late nineteenth century and since?

As immigration to the United States greatly expanded, so did the foreign-language press. By the 1880s, there were nearly eight hundred foreign-language newspapers; by World War I there were close to 1300 dailies and weeklies. Most of these were small businesses that, like neighborhood restaurants, were quickly begun and often failed just as quickly, but some lasted. There were newspapers in Danish, German, Italian, and Yiddish that lasted more than a century.

The largest foreign-language press was German. In the late nineteenth and early twentieth century there were even German-speaking labor unions and German-language labor newspapers to serve them, more than one hundred published between 1870 and 1900. A general circulation German paper, the New York *Staats-Zeitung*, had a circulation of 90,000 in the 1890s—making it at the time the largest German-language newspaper in the world. But the German-language press was all but wiped out in World War I when the German-American community strongly opposed America's entry into the war on the side of Germany's enemies. When the United States declared war on Germany, the German-language newspapers affirmed their loyalty to America, but they still lost subscribers and advertisers who feared the enmity of their neighbors for everything overtly German. Moreover, the Trading with the Enemy Act of 1917 required that publishers of foreign-language news articles about the war file translations with their local postmasters before publication. This was costly and forced some of the newspapers out of business. Others lost mailing privileges when they were seen as critics of US government policy. Under wartime legislation, the government charged some editors with disloyalty.

A foreign-language press survived into the 1940s, when there were still 1000 newspapers and magazines in thirty-eight languages, but the foreign-language press did not regain the prominence it had in 1910. Still, with immigration growing again after immigration reform in the 1960s, and notably new immigration from Latin America and from Asia, foreign-language papers serving new immigrant communities revived and expanded. Notable also is the emergence of Spanish-language broadcasting.

How did slaves and later free African Americans get their news?

It was not easy for the African slaves to get news. Few were literate and state laws in most Southern states from the 1830s on made it a crime to teach slaves to read. On the eve of the Civil War, literacy among black Americans was about 5 to 10%. But that changed with emancipation. Schools sprang up and literacy rose to 30% by 1880, and 77% by 1920. Not only elementary schools but more than eighty black colleges began in the two decades after the Civil War. This rapid growth of education was possible because free Negroes in the South—about 260,000 in 1860—managed to establish instruction, often through their churches. Some states—Louisiana, Kentucky, North Carolina—never banned schools for free Negroes. After emancipation, there was a corps of literate African Americans equipped to help the former slaves.

After World War I, the "Great Migration" of blacks from South to North proceeded rapidly. It was driven by a depressed agricultural economy as well as by intensified racial tension, including the rise of the Ku Klux Klan. It was also encouraged by the circulation in the South of African American newspapers from the North. This included from 1905 the *Chicago Defender* (a weekly until it became a daily in 1956, returning to weekly publication in 2003), which "except for the Bible, was probably the most influential publication in Afro-America," as historian James Danky writes. The *Defender* took an aggressively antiracist stance. It circulated widely in the South. It posted notices of job opportunities in the North, and it organized clubs to help the migrants make their transition to urban life. It mixed sensational coverage of corruption and vice along with strong editorials against segregation and lynching and coverage of other serious political fare.

Another prominent African American newspaper, the *Pittsburgh Courier* (1907–1966), reached at its height a circulation of 350,000. The *Courier* promoted the "Double V" campaign during World War II, urging victory in the war against Germany and Japan and, equally, victory at home against racial discrimination.

The black press grew for a few years after the war but in the 1950s faltered badly. Dailies became weeklies, weeklies disappeared, and by the end of the 1960s a once thriving part of American journalism had become a ghost of itself. It did not secure the kind of advertising base that sustained the mainstream press. In many African American homes, the black newspaper was a "second" paper, and advertisers could still reach black Americans in the general circulation newspapers, while black businesses with local or neighborhood clientele were often not inspired to support the black press. As civil rights became increasingly a top news story in the mid-1950s and after, even in the mainstream press that had long neglected the black community or treated it disparagingly, it became more possible for readers to follow this important news in the general media and for advertisers to reach African Americans without buying space in African American papers.

Did the "yellow press" drive America into war with Spain in 1898?

The textbooks have long said so, but they are wrong. The "yellows" were apparently so named because the two leading practitioners of sensationalism in the news, Joseph Pulitzer's *New York World* (which Pulitzer had bought in 1883) and William Randolph Hearst's *New York Journal* (which Hearst purchased in 1895) both ran a comic strip called "The Yellow Kid." Pulitzer and Hearst competed for the mass audience, and they were willing to be sensational to attract it. That included puffing up news of Spanish atrocities or alleged atrocities in Cuba. But the question remains: what influence did these newspapers have? Consider some relevant facts:

1. Both papers were ardent supporters of the Democratic Party. In the run-up to the Spanish-American War, the White House and the Congress were both controlled by Republicans.
2. Warmaking was a decision of the President and the Congress. The Senate was elected in those days not by popular vote but by the state legislatures. Senators therefore had to think about maintaining the support of their party, but they had little reason to worry about public opinion. They were well insulated from it. The President was more vulnerable—but, in 1896, he was still not *very* vulnerable. Republicans had controlled the White House from 1860 through 1896 with the exception of Grover Cleveland's two election victories in 1884 and 1892. In 1896 Ohio Republican William McKinley won the election for President. He carried New York—the only state where the *New York World* and the *New York Journal* had influence—by an overwhelming 58% to 39% against William Jennings Bryan.
3. President McKinley's staff prepared a regular news summary for him, but it rarely included anything from the *World* or the *Journal*. Neither paper was taken seriously in Washington; the yellow press, in fact, was the butt of White House jokes. Historians of the McKinley administration have simply not found letters, memos, or other commentary to suggest newspaper enthusiasm for war had any impact on McKinley's decision to go to war.

So why do we hear so often that the yellow press pushed the country into war? It appears that this became a consensus position among historians after World War I. World War I featured a massive outpouring of propaganda. Some popular historians, sharing a growing alarm, criticized propaganda for propelling America into a European war they believed we should have stayed out of, and they read their suspicion of propaganda back into the Spanish-American War. But in World War I both British and German propaganda efforts were centrally coordinated by the British and German governments—and so was American propaganda after 1917 when the United States entered the war. In 1898, propagandistic influences were uncoordinated and, so far as can be determined, unavailing. Pulitzer and Hearst loom large in the history of journalism, but they had no detectable influence on American foreign policy.

How did American newspapers, largely identified with political parties for most of the nineteenth century, come to pride themselves on "objectivity"?

You can easily come upon misleading answers to this rather complicated question. The two most often repeated wrong answers are:

> The telegraph did it. When it became common for reporters to send news back to the home office by telegram (beginning with the US–Mexico War soon after the electronic telegraph was invented, and coming into wider use during and after the Civil War) it became important to write *brief* dispatches. The longer the telegram, the more the newspaper paid for it. Adjectives disappeared. Opinion was squeezed out. Basic facts remained.

So the story goes. But most newspaper writing remained florid and fulsome long after the telegraph was in broad use. News style became gradually leaner in the late nineteenth century—but then so did prose in fiction, none of it transmitted by wire. There is no evidence that the telegraph was basic to the transformation of news style, although there is no reason to doubt that telegrams offered a model of how a lot of information could be transmitted tersely.

> Economics did it. Newspapers sought to make more money by appealing to both Democratic and Republican readers. With high-speed presses, abundant paper from wood-pulping, and Mergenthaler typecasting machines (1886), plus rapid urbanization and a growing and increasingly concentrated advertising market, partisanship became economically irrational. Why not appeal to readers across party lines and make a lot more money?

This seems like common sense. But nineteenth-century publishers started their own papers or bought papers not only to make money but also to establish political influence. When Joseph Pulitzer bought the *New York World* in 1883, he wanted to make it a "schoolhouse," as he put it, and he was personally most interested in the editorial page. When William Randolph Hearst bought the *New York Journal* in 1895, he wanted his paper to support the Democratic Party and to influence it. Both of these titans of the newspaper industry served—albeit briefly—as Democrats from New York in the US Congress, Pulitzer from 1885–1886 and Hearst 1903–1907.

When Tennessee newspaperman Adolph Ochs bought the *New York Times* in 1896, he did not try to compete directly with Pulitzer and Hearst but to differentiate himself from them and the other dailies in the city. In articulating his philosophy for the newspaper, he said he would "intensify its devotion to the cause of sound money and tariff reform" and would support "advocacy of the lowest tax consistent with good government, and no more government than is absolutely necessary to protect society." Today's *New York Times* seems to have forgotten this part of Ochs's three-paragraph credo and routinely quotes only the publisher's assertion in the same charter-setting statment that the paper would "give the news impartially, without fear or favor, regardless of any party, sect, or interest involved."

So where did "objectivity" come from? There is no single force at work here. Multiple factors mattered. In the United States and slightly later in Britain, news organizations placed growing emphasis on what have been called "fact-centered discursive practices." That is, not only did newspapers focus more intently on getting the facts and getting them right, but reporters inaugurated new tools for doing so. Most important of these was interviewing. American reporters were the first in the world to make interviewing a chief method for gathering news, and they would go on, particularly during World War I, to show their European colleagues how to do it, although by that time some British reporters had fully adopted the practice. As the ranks of reporters increased in the growing cities of the late nineteenth century, reporters developed a comradeship and a devotion to one another separate from—and sometimes even hostile to—their employment relationships to the publishers who paid them. They gathered after work in the same bars and pubs. They established clubs. Specialized trade journals catered to their interests. Some reporters thought that journalism was a temporary job, a way station to fame and fortune in literature, but others increasingly came to understand themselves to be reporters. Reporting facts became their professional pride.

Reporters were part of an increasingly fact-minded, science-minded, and antipolitical cultural mood. Political reform efforts based on distrust of establishment party politics in the 1880s (civil service reform) and the 1890s (the secret ballot; the establishment of nonpartisan municipal elections where candidates were not allowed to identify themselves by party on the ballot; the passage in many states of laws to allow citizens to vote directly on legislative proposals by "initiative," bypassing the party-controlled state legislatures) were part of a mood of independence from parties. Reformers believed that political leadership should rise above partisanship and be dedicated to the technical tasks of making government work.

These developments led journalism on the path toward what we might recognize as "objective" reporting, but it did not for the most part lead journalists to clearly articulate "objectivity" as an ethical value until after World War I. The war brought on waves of propaganda activity not only among the European combatants but in the US government as well, once it declared war. Moreover, about the same time and increasingly in the years following the war, "public relations" became an industry and public relations specialists were becoming more commonly employed by businesses, by government agencies, and by nonprofit institutions like universities and hospitals. Reporters quickly felt themselves deluged by outsiders eager to have their perspectives on events represented directly or indirectly in the pages of the newspapers. Journalists complained that journalism schools, still very new, were churning out more public relations specialists than reporters. It was at this point that journalists, recognizing the efforts of governments, businesses, and others to plant stories in the press to enhance their reputation, power, or profit, asserted that they would not be swayed by any of it. With interested parties seeking control of newspaper content, the reporters insisted that they would bow to no one and nothing but to their own ethic of disinterested, fact-based, balanced, and fair-minded reporting.

This new model of professional journalism, often called "objective" reporting at the time and after, was further institutionalized and maintained because it served newspaper editors as a kind of discipline for directing and controlling their increasingly large staffs of young reporters learning the trade on the job. College education was rare among reporters in the 1920s, 1930s, and 1940s. Newspapers were their own training schools and "objectivity"—sometimes called "balance" or "fairness"—was a useful pedagogy.

Many things in human affairs have multiple, conjoined causes. The professionalization of journalism and the emergence of an ethical code and set of work practices called "objectivity" is one of them.

Is adherence to the value of "objectivity" the heart of what it means to be a "professional" in journalism?

No, although US journalists and scholars of journalism often speak as if these terms are inseparable.

In journalism, it is possible to institute norms of objectivity without establishing a pervasive culture in news organizations that encourages them. This happened in Brazil in the 1950s. Brazilian newspapers until then had operated largely under the influence of the French newspaper model—a more essayistic, literary, philosophical, and politicized model of journalism. But, beginning at Rio de Janeiro's *Diario Carioca* in the early 1950s, Brazilian newspapers came under US influence. *Diario Carioca's* news writing editor (Pompeu de Sousa), editor-in-chief (Danton Jobim), and chief of reporters (Luis Paulistano) led the reforms, Sousa and Jobim having served during World War II in the United States in a program set up by the US government to influence Latin American politics and society.

After the war, these leaders of *Diario Carioca* pushed for the American model, arguing that the French model treated journalism not as a business but as a priesthood. The French emphasis on journalism as a political and literary pursuit was elitist, they argued, and Jobim wrote that the US style better addressed its reader as "a friend who talks to him, sharing his ideas and sentiments." The reformers dictated that news stories begin with a US-style summary lead and follow it with the "inverted pyramid," providing the most important information first and proceeding to other information in order of decreasing importance. A typical French opening, one that offered moral commentary to introduce a story, was abandoned. The reformers not only preached these new rules but enforced them by hiring new reporters with no previous experience in journalism—"zero-kilometer" journalists. And then they controlled the new reporters by placing authority at the copy desk, not in the autonomy of individual reporters. This is what Brazilian scholars have called "authoritarian modernization," a kind of revolution from above that produced "professionalization without professionalism." In other words, it enabled newspapers to establish practices of objectivity without instilling in reporters a moral urgency about it.

If "objectivity" is not the heart of professionalism in journalism, what (if anything) is?

We are not suggesting that norms of objectivity, fairness, detachment, truth-seeking, or nonpartisanship are unrelated to professionalism. But professionalism is a multilayered term. While there is no agreed-upon classic definition, it is frequently said that an occupation is a profession when it is so organized that (1) members have a high degree of autonomy in their work and in judgments about the quality of their work, uncoerced by the state or the marketplace; (2) members have formal codes of ethics they take seriously or informal values that orient them to public service; and (3) while not all occupations that professionalize are "learned professions," they all normally take pride in the mastery of a set of skills that require significant study or experience to master.

Most sociological definitions focus on the points listed above, often emphasizing also that members of the profession control access to membership. You can see at once that, in these terms, journalism can scarcely be called a profession at all. Access to a position, even a very high position as an editor or producer, is not exclusive—no specific training is required, no college degree is required, there is no exam to pass, and there is no "license" required to practice. Access to important inner circles may require further approval, however; for instance, accreditation as a White House correspondent admitted to presidential press conferences requires obtaining a congressional press pass. This is under the control of the

Standing Committee of Correspondents, a group elected by the accredited reporters. Still, having a congressional press pass does not put you in a very exclusive club—there are more than 2,000 reporters who are so accredited and who are eligible to cover the White House.

Journalism is "professional" in that it is a full-time, white-collar occupation that today invariably calls for a college degree (although not necessarily a degree in journalism); that increasingly depends on mastering an assortment of technical skills; and that requires that one demonstrate wide-ranging curiosity and a capacity to work across different domains of human activity with agility and speed. An institutional array of verbal praise from editors and peers, salary rewards and advancement in responsibility, and well-publicized prizes awarded by national committees of widely esteemed journalists reinforce a sense of integrity and a belief that journalism is a public service. That sense that journalism is a calling dedicated to public service is encouraged but not enforced. This general ethic of service may include a commitment to holding power to account (by "speaking truth to power") but it may not; it may include dedication to seeking as best as one can to be "objective" but it may not; it may include a sense of responsibility to a local community or to a set of devoted readers but it may not.

Is it true that Mark Twain, Theodore Dreiser, Stephen Crane, Willa Cather, Ernest Hemingway, and other famous novelists were all reporters before they became famous as novelists?

Yes. Many people who aspire to be novelists began their writing careers as journalists. The thirteen-year-old Anne Frank had exactly this in mind for herself, and it is hard to believe that someone so full of life and so gifted at writing as a child would not have accomplished what she set out to do had the Nazis not murdered her. She wrote in her diary about "the big question, will I ever be able to write something great, will I ever become a journalist or a writer?"

There are many others, too—Martha Gellhorn, Jack London, Margaret Mitchell (*Gone With the Wind*), Tom Wolfe—who wrote for newspapers or magazines before turning to fiction. John Steinbeck, already a published novelist, wrote a series of pieces on the Okie migrant camps of California for the *San Francisco News* before writing his most celebrated book, also about the migrants, *The Grapes of Wrath*. Across the Atlantic, George Orwell worked as a journalist, as had Charles Dickens a century earlier, and Daniel Defoe, a century before Dickens.

Journalism offers an aspiring writer much more than a paycheck (not that pay is a small matter). It is common advice to young writers to "write what you know." But how do you acquire firsthand knowledge, not textbook knowledge, of real life? The distinctive feature of the novel, as novelist and critic Mary McCarthy observed, is "its concern with the actual world, the world of fact, of the verifiable, of figures, even, and statistics." What unites writers as different as Austen and Tolstoy, Dostoevsky and Proust, Dickens and Joyce is "a deep love of fact, of the empiric element in experience. . . . The stable ingredient present in all novels in various mixtures and proportions but always in fairly heavy dosage is fact."

How do you learn the world—and at close hand, close enough to absorb the language, the color, the fabric of somebody else's experience? Journalism is one very good way. It has its own limits. Those limits may have grown in the past several decades as reporters do more of their work from their desks and computers, less from going out into the world. What journalists have proudly called "shoe leather reporting" is not as clearly the heart of the job of reporting as it once was. But it has not gone away. And as news reporting has come to cover a wider range of human experiences, moving away from a primary or nearly exclusive emphasis on politics and government, there have been more and more opportunities for reporters to learn the world, and to do so on topics that could lend themselves to successful fiction.

Who were the "muckrakers"?

The term "muckraking" dates to 1906 when President Theodore Roosevelt criticized journalists for tearing down the country by their insistent emphasis on corruption and scandal. These writers were, he said, like "the Man with the Muck-rake" in John Bunyan's seventeenth-century spiritual classic, *Pilgrim's Progress*, who focused exclusively on filth rather than salvation. Roosevelt insisted to his friends in the press that his target was just William Randolph Hearst's newspaper and magazine empire but not the responsible critical investigations in leading magazines like *McClure's* where Lincoln Steffens, Ida Tarbell, Ray Stannard Baker, and others published. Roosevelt was particularly upset by the appearance in Hearst's *The Cosmopolitan* magazine of David Graham Phillips' nine-part series, "The Treason of the Senate." Soon thereafter, Roosevelt gave an off-the-record talk to journalists at a private club, but word got out that he planned to deliver it again as a public address. His muckraker friends urged him not to, but Roosevelt went ahead anyway to both praise and condemn investigative journalism. Critical reports could be "indispensable" but could likewise be "potent forces for evil" when sensational and untruthful.

Roosevelt's praise was quickly forgotten; the critique stuck. So did the term "muckraker." The original muckrakers invariably wrote for magazines or published their muckraking work in books. Muckraking was not a notable feature of the newspapers of the early 1900s. Criticism there was a-plenty in the newspapers, but it was typically motivated by and infused with political partisanship. It was not driven by a pride in investigative finesse or professional virtue. But even in magazines the heyday of muckraking was brief. The most famous of the muckrakers wrote for *McClure's* and a handful of other upscale national magazines. The leading writers at *McClure's* left the magazine in 1906, bought *The American* magazine, and hoped to continue their muckraking ways there. The effort fizzled. Despite Roosevelt's criticism, the influence of these magazine writers stemmed in large part from the reforming energy of the Roosevelt administration itself. Roosevelt fueled muckraking. The end of the Roosevelt presidency in 1909 was also in many ways the end of the era of the muckrakers.

Years later, Leonard Downie, Jr., then a young editor at the *Washington Post*, fresh from working on the team that had edited Woodward and Bernstein, would write *The New Muckrakers* (1976) with chapters on different contemporary muckrakers. His central examples were primarily newspaper writers—Bernstein and Woodward, syndicated columnist Jack Anderson, Seymour Hersh, David Barlett and James Steele at the *Philadelphia Inquirer*, Mike Baxter and Jim Savage at the *Miami Herald*, along with Bruce Brugmann at the *San Francisco Bay Guardian* (a weekly), and Carey McWilliams, editor of *The Nation* (also a weekly). In terms of constructing a self-identified field of investigative reporting with a coherent and enduring legacy, the "new muckraking" that took off in the late 1960s had a much more pervasive and lasting influence on journalism than the original muckrakers.

What the original investigative era contributed was a shining example and, thanks to Roosevelt, a name. Still when muckraking became institutionalized in the 1970s, it did so under a different name, the term "investigative reporting." And what exactly is that? "The only workable definition of an investigative reporter is a reporter who spends a lot of time doing investigations," according to a 1976 textbook on the subject. Or, as the authors say a few pages later, "Investigative reporting, then, is simply the reporting of concealed information." Others place emphasis on a specific intent in investigative journalism—calling it "the journalism of outrage." They hold that it is distinctive in seeking to provoke indignation in readers or viewers; it is not just a form of gathering news but also of policing threats to public morality, exposing shortcomings in society in the hope of restitution and reform.

This second coming of muckraking, more than the first, found its home in America's daily newspapers and the culture of its newsrooms. It was in 1967 that *Newsday* became the first newspaper to establish an investigative "team" of reporters to do nothing but investigative work. The Associated Press created a similar "special assignment" team the same year. The *Chicago Tribune* followed in 1968. The *Boston Globe* adopted the same model in 1970 with its "spotlight" team. In 1968, *60 Minutes* took the investigative reporting ideal to television for CBS. Nearly fifty years later, it is still a staple of Sunday night television and the longest running prime time show in any genre in US television history.

In 1975 a national organization of investigative journalists was established, Investigative Reporters and Editors. It continues to offer education and training in investigative journalism and moral and social support for its members. "The journalism of outrage" has become an enduring ideal in American journalism, persisting in shrinking newspaper newsrooms and being adopted with enthusiasm in many online start-ups..

What kind of education did journalists typically have in the past? When—and why—did formal course work in and schools of journalism develop?

Until the mid-nineteenth century, one typically became a doctor or a lawyer through apprenticeship, not through schooling. In the United States, law schools and medical schools became the primary path to professional practice only in the late nineteenth century. Formal state licensing became commonplace about the same time.

In journalism, in the United States, there has never been state licensing. Nor has formal training been required; journalists until the late twentieth century typically learned the trade on the job. Courses in journalism began to be offered at a few colleges in the late nineteenth century but no school dedicated to journalism education existed until the University of Missouri established its school in 1908. The idea of a college education for journalists had been under discussion for some years by then, and Joseph Pulitzer wrote a lengthy piece in the *North American Review* in 1904 advocating formal college-level journalism training. He did more than write about it; he donated in his will the money that made possible a School of Journalism at Columbia. It opened its doors in 1914. Many other schools—although no other "Ivy League" schools—would follow. The heart of US journalism education developed in public universities—from Texas to Wisconsin and Minnesota; from the University of California, Berkeley to the University of Maryland and University of North Carolina. Private universities have been much less likely to establish journalism programs, Columbia and Northwestern University's Medill School of Journalism being the most prominent exceptions.

Journalists in the past did not apply any sort of abstract or conceptual knowledge to their work. The expectation was that good reporting requires skill in writing and a "nose for news"—the ability to recognize when a set of events constitutes a "story" and a knack for getting to the heart of it. Frequently, but not always, journalists were expected to have social skills to enable them to establish rapport with a wide range of possible sources or to have the courage to breach ordinary rules of civility by raising challenging, even hostile questions on sensitive issues.

None of this is anything like the kind of knowledge one is supposed to master in a medical school or a law school. Some journalists, especially in recent decades, do acquire specialized knowledge, perhaps courses or even a degree in law to cover the judicial system, perhaps some background in science to cover science and medicine, perhaps even a medical degree. But these are the exceptions. There are some efforts, but the majority of them less than a decade old, to train students in "data journalism."

The US led the way in developing organized journalism education in colleges and universities. In Europe, formal journalism education is largely a post-1945 phenomenon. In some countries, like Germany, some journalism education takes place in universities but some takes place also in schools run by large media organizations themselves.

There is no licensing of journalists in democracies. The international free press organization, "Article 19" (named after the free expression provision of the Universal Declaration of Human Rights) observes that international human rights agreements oppose licensing or registration of journalists as a violation of rights to free expression. Even requiring educational qualifications for practicing journalism is generally regarded among human rights advocates as impinging on free speech. However, there are more limited rules in many countries, including the United States, that regulate reporters' access to government buildings and high-level news conferences, or other settings where limited space is a genuine practical concern. In these cases, access may be governed by journalists themselves, organized through their own associations, like the White House Correspondents' Association.

What is a Pulitzer Prize?

The Pulitzer Prize is the most prestigious of all awards or prizes for American journalists. The Pulitzer Prizes were established as part of a bequest made by Joseph Pulitzer, the Hungarian-born American reporter and editor who bought the *New York World* in 1883 and turned it into one of the largest, most innovative, and most lucrative newspapers anywhere. After his death, as part of his gift to Columbia University to establish a School of Journalism, he provided the funds for the Pulitzer Prizes.

There are Pulitzer prizes for history, biography or autobiography, general non-fiction, drama, poetry, fiction, and music. In journalism, there are fourteen prizes—thirteen that go to individuals or groups of individuals for work in specific journalism fields, from editorial writing to editorial cartooning, from breaking news photography to investigative reporting to feature writing. The prize for public service is awarded to a news organization rather than to an individual journalist.

The self-perpetuating Pulitzer board has full power to maintain the prizes as it determines, although the prizes are officially presented to recipients by the president of Columbia University who, along with the dean of the Columbia Journalism School, are ex officio members of the board. Sometimes the board makes significant changes in the awards—adding the prize in music in 1943, expanding the music award in the 1960s from classical music composition to jazz composition, inaugurating a prize in "explanatory journalism" in 1985. Since 2006 the Pulitzer board has welcomed online elements of newspaper submissions and since 2009 has invited submissions from online-only news organizations. In 2013, a small, online-only news organization founded in 2007, Inside Climate News, won the Pulitzer for national reporting.

Other awards celebrate achievements in radio and television news, notably the Alfred I. DuPont-Columbia University awards—established in 1942 and administered by Columbia since 1968—and the George Foster Peabody Awards, established in 1940 and administered through the Grady College of Journalism, University of Georgia. The National Magazine Awards, established by the American Society of Magazine Editors in 1966, and also administered through the Columbia Journalism School, recognize news and public affairs magazine excellence. There are other prestigious national awards for journalism as well as awards chosen by state and local press clubs and press associations.

These various changes in the Pulitzer awards have done nothing to diminish and have almost certainly enhanced Joseph Pulitzer's original intention of creating awards that contribute to recognizing journalism as a professional pursuit in the public interest. Pulitzer wrote earnestly in his 1904 essay: "Our Republic and its press will rise or fall together. An able, disinterested, public-spirited press, with trained intelligence to know the right and courage to do it, can preserve that public virtue without which popular government is a sham and a mockery. A cynical, mercenary, demagogic press will produce in time a people as base as itself. The power to mould the future of the Republic will be in the hands of the journalists of future generations."

How do you win a Pulitzer Prize in journalism? There are different criteria for different prizes. Sig Gissler, the executive director of the Pulitzers from 2002 to 2014, told us that winners in public service, investigative reporting, and national reporting are usually marked by "deep-digging reportage and evocative storytelling (using all available tools, including video)." Jurors also give weight to "results and impact. Did the stories produce meaningful change?" With breaking news, jurors look for "coherent balance under deadline pressure. They look for immediacy—swift, accurate coverage especially during the first 24 to 48 hours after a story breaks, with demonstrated examples of real-time reporting." Still, even for breaking news, jurors "also seek coverage that, over several days, places an event in context."

Is it unethical for journalists to be or to become friends with the people they write about?

Is it okay for reporters and columnists who write about politicians to have dinner with them? Play touch football with them? Give them advice? Write their speeches?

The answer has changed through the years. In the nineteenth century, reporters covering Washington routinely served as clerks of congressional committees, drawing income from one or more news organizations and the US Congress at the same time. This was standard practice. More rarely, but still widely known at the time, some of the clerk/reporters made additional money selling secrets to fellow journalists.

Lest we imagine that this intimacy between reporters and their sources disappeared as we moved from the bad nineteenth century to the good, more professional twentieth century, consider the behavior of one of Washington's consummate insiders, the syndicated columnist Joseph Alsop. Alsop (1910–1989) was a prominent journalist who, as it happens, was Eleanor Roosevelt's cousin. At one point, in 1939, working on a piece for the *Saturday Evening Post* on American foreign policy, he contacted Eleanor to arrange an interview with President Roosevelt. He assured her that he approved of FDR's foreign policy, that he would submit a draft to the president for approval before sending anything to the magazine, and that he would conceal the president's help on the story. In the end the *Post* rejected the long piece, but Alsop published it all as a book.

Like Alsop, Walter Lippmann was an insider, a confidant of the rich and powerful. In 1940 he gave political advice to Wendell Willkie, the Republican candidate for president running against FDR. In 1945, Lippmann, along with *New York Times* reporter James Reston, met with Republican Senator Arthur Vandenberg (Michigan) and advised him to abandon his isolationism if he had serious presidential aspirations (which he did). The two journalists teamed up to write a speech for Vandenberg that he delivered in the Senate to great acclaim—and some of that acclaim came from Lippmann in his syndicated newspaper column and from Reston, reporting in the *Times* that that the speech was "wise" and "statesmanlike."

Alsop, Lippmann, and some others achieved, or assumed, a priestly stature in American journalism—above the fray of politics, at least in their own minds, but eager participants in it. They were not objective reporters, but do priestly journalists serve the public good, too? And commentators and critics—whether of music or theater or politics? And even jesters? Think of the role that newspaper columnist and radio commentator Will Rogers played in the in the 1920s and 1930s or the public role of Jon Stewart and Stephen Colbert since Stewart began hosting Comedy Central's "The Daily Show" in 1999. Just as there are quite different styles of doctoring or of teaching, and not just one way to brilliantly practice medicine or to instruct and inspire as a teacher, there is not just one acceptable model of how journalists should serve the public in journalism.

At the same time, American journalists have grown hostile to insider journalism when it blurs the line between reporting politics and doing politics or between reporting in the interest of public understanding and participating in the formation of public policy. Writing editorials, writing "opinion" pieces like regular columnists on the "op-ed" page, writing in-depth news analysis, and writing daily breaking news stories are all different but legitimate forms of journalism. Writing a politician's speeches is not journalism; writing a news story or an opinion column about a candidate's speech that you have written without acknowledging that you wrote it violates an implicit public trust that journalism depends on.

Why did radio not kill off newspapers?

New media challenge the old. New technologies have specific features or what have been called "affordances" that do not duplicate previous technologies. By the same token, the older technologies have affordances that the new ones do not reproduce. The new ones do not do just the *same* as the old, faster or better; they do something *like* the old but not exactly.

Print journalists certainly feared radio. Some of the more prosperous newspapers handled their anxiety by buying radio stations themselves. But many other newspapers felt radio was unfair competition, especially when wire service news—produced by newspapers—became readily available to radio so that the papers sometimes were scooped by their own stories on radio.

But radio did not have some of the important features people enjoyed with newspapers. You did not need to make an appointment for a certain hour and minute to get news from your newspaper. In the United States, at a time when most major cities had two or more daily newspapers, each newspaper typically had a political affiliation or political leaning, something readers felt comfortable with and that helped them feel connected with the newspaper. The headline style of radio news, in contrast, did not produce a personal identification. Of course, radio offered an immediacy greater than newspapers and the intimacy of the human voice, but newspapers had features that radio could not duplicate—among other things, newspapers printed photographs. You could see in a newspaper but not in radio what Roosevelt looked like, or Hoover, or Hitler.

Perhaps the best insight about the distinctive affordances of the newspaper came from interviews conducted during a long New York newspaper strike in 1945–1946. Researchers asked people during the strike what not having their newspapers meant to them. It turned out that people were pretty vague about what subject matter they missed—stories they wanted to follow in the news that then were suddenly cut off. But they vividly described the sense of loss in their daily routines. Reading the paper was part of a daily ritual, often at a specific time of day. It was a pleasure and a comfort that fit into a pattern of everyday activity and offered a familiarity that radio did not replace.

And why did television not destroy newspapers?

Television did not kill off newspapers either, but it contributed to the death of the newspapers that published in the afternoons rather than the mornings. The number of dailies declined significantly in the 1950s and 1960s—and has fairly steadily declined ever since. With rare exceptions, it was the afternoon papers that vanished most quickly. This was not that people simply preferred TV to print but that television was integrated into a broad shift in how people lived their lives.

It was part of the rapid suburbanization of American cities. When people left their offices, factories, and warehouses at the end of the working day, they increasingly left the city behind, often on long commutes, increasingly by car. The whole pattern of living changed and the afternoon newspaper did not fit into it so neatly as before. Meanwhile, the signature evening television news broadcast provided a substitute good enough to make the afternoon newspaper seem to many an unnecessary family expense.

By 2000, throughout the countries of the European Union, according to the Eurobarometer data of the European Commission, more people watched television news every day than read a newspaper daily—except in Sweden where the newspapers had a slight edge. In southern Europe, the TV advantage was great—83% in Italy saw TV news daily, only 30% read a newspaper daily; in France it was 62% and 26% respectively. In northern Europe and in Britain, the TV edge was less dramatic—68% to 59% in Germany, 71% to 47% in Britain, 79% to 67% in Finland.

Why have many democracies invested public funds in broadcasting?

The world's most influential model for broadcast news is the British Broadcasting Corporation (BBC). It employs around five thousand journalists and maintains some forty foreign bureaus. (The *New York Times*, in comparison, employs about one thousand journalists. CBS News has about 150 journalists on staff.) Other European nations also have substantial public broadcasting systems with much larger audiences than public broadcasting in the United States—including the Nordic countries, Germany, France, and others.

In a 2011 study of public broadcasting in ten European democracies plus the United States, Canada, Japan, Australia, and New Zealand, researchers calculated that the United States invested less than four dollars per capita per year in public radio and television. The next lowest investors were Canada and New Zealand at $30 per capita and Australia at $34. Britain spends $90 per capita while at the high end Denmark, Norway, and Germany all provide over $130 per capita.

The BBC began in the 1920s and received its royal charter as a public corporation in 1926. Its influential first director, John Reith, did not believe its news service should provide propaganda for the government, but he did believe that, in both news and entertainment, radio should knit together a common culture for Britain. One acquaintance said Reith spoke "as though he was in charge of the national well-being." That is exactly what he took the BBC's job to be. He held that it was the BBC's responsibility "to carry into the greatest possible number of homes everything that is best in every department of human knowledge, endeavor, and achievement, and to avoid things which are, or may be, hurtful." As early as 1923, Reith urged King George V to use the BBC to address the nation on Christmas or New Year's. Only in 1932 did the king finally comply. By 1934 he addressed the audience in his Christmas message as "the members of our worldwide family," establishing an annual ritual that continues to this day.

At first, the BBC's charter forbade discussion or coverage of controversy on air. Although this ban was removed in 1928, a genuine political independence in news coverage began only in the mid-1950s when rivalry with the newly established commercial broadcasting service, ITV, "had the effect of detaching the BBC from the apron strings of the state," as BBC historian Paddy Scannell put it.

Whereas in most countries newspapers and magazines preceded national sovereignty, broadcasting appeared after the establishment of independent nation-states or was quickly appropriated by the first postcolonial governments. In most societies, less gun-shy of central governmental authority than the United States, this has led to powerful state broadcasting. It has also produced in most cases successful efforts to maintain what the British call an "arm's-length" distance between the government in power and the quasi-independent boards that govern broadcasting. The legislation or government orders establishing public broadcasting in contemporary democracies all promise the broadcaster substantial or effectively complete editorial independence from the state.

The United States has some entities like its National Science Foundation, National Institutes of Health, and National Endowment for the Humanities that, though funded by the federal government, preserve normal scientific "peer review" as the primary decision-making mechanism for establishing scientific research priorities and making grants to scholars. The United States sought to emulate other democracies in setting up the Public Broadcasting Service in 1967 but comparable funding never followed.

Why is there a Freedom of Information Act—and does it do any good?

In 1966 the United States enacted a law granting "any person" (any person in the world, of any age, for any reason) the right to request information held by the federal government—and the right to take the government to court if the request is denied. The first nation to have a law of this sort was Sweden—in 1766. But the American act brought the idea into the modern age. The American version became the model for many other nations that came to adopt similar laws in the past half century.

The American law—the Freedom of Information Act (or "FOIA")—bold as it is, has two notable limitations. First, it does not cover the Congress or the courts. Only agencies of the executive branch of government are covered by the law. Second, the law lists nine "exemptions"—conditions that justify the government in refusing to release information to the requester. Among these conditions are that disclosure of the requested information bears on national security; that it violates the privacy rights of an individual; that it exposes legitimate trade secrets; or that it exposes deliberation (rather than final decisions) inside an executive agency. In this last case, the rationale for the exemption is that if internal deliberations were subject to FOIA requests, participants would censor themselves; open and unrestrained discussion would be constrained at exactly the moments when free-flowing discussion is most crucial to good decisions.

FOIA has changed over time. Amendments to the law in 1974 did much to make the law tighter and tougher—for instance, it set time limits for agencies to respond to requesters. That made the prospect that a requester could sue when information is refused much more likely.

Where did this law come from? It was not something the American founders ever discussed. And while it became law in the 1960s, it came out of a legislative effort that began in 1955 in the midst of the Cold War. At that time, several forces converged to give it traction. The executive branch of government was rapidly growing and so was the eagerness with which the executive classified information and kept not only the press and the public at arm's length but also the Congress. Both Republicans and Democrats in the Congress wanted to regain some control over the executive.

Moreover, there was an available Cold War rhetoric conveniently at hand for slamming efforts to withhold information from the American public. John Moss, the California Democrat who chaired a House of Representatives subcommittee on governmental information, regularly attacked the executive branch for building a "paper curtain" between the government and the public. This played on the familiar Cold War phrase, "the iron curtain," that shielded the Soviet Union and eastern Europe from information flowing in from the West. To accuse the US government of building a "paper curtain" was to suggest that its information policies were distastefully Soviet-like. There was every effort to credit American government and society with an open mind, a tolerance for difference of opinion, and a scientific spirit. "The Americans" were portrayed as everything that totalitarian societies like the Soviet Union were not.

The result was that John Moss and his allies in the House, the Senate, and the press corps successfully and repeatedly embarrassed the Eisenhower administration and later the Kennedy administration for withholding information where there was no reason to do so, other than bureaucratic habit or bureaucratic arrogance. Eventually, Congress approved FOIA, and a reluctant Lyndon Johnson signed the act into law.

Not everybody loved FOIA. It drew criticism from the beginning. Consumer activist Ralph Nader called it the "Freedom *From* Information Act." Even later, after several amendments were passed to strengthen it and streamline its use, reporters, historians, and others who attempted to use it have found it slow and frustrating. It affords the government all kinds of ways to defer and delay and, even when releasing information, to release far less than requested. A *New York Times* correspondent in 2008 called it a "cruel joke." Sarah Cohen, then a *Washington Post* reporter, testifying before Congress on the subject in 2011, observed, "I have never received a final response to a FOIA (request) within the required time frame. Some reporters joke about sending birthday cards to their FOIAs, as the response times are measured in years, not days."

Still, Cohen listed many important stories that, in her words, "could not have been done without access to records locked inside technological and physical file cabinets throughout the government." For her, the FOIA process was frustrating—and indispensable. It has also been one of the great legislative exports of the United States—today there are more than one hundred freedom of information laws around the world. Some have advantages and efficiencies greater than the US law does—say, covering the legislature as well as the executive, or requiring faster turnaround, or providing a means of rapid response to adjudicate FOIA requests if they are denied.

What was New Journalism?

Nobody, I mean, nobody had ever seen the world fresh, when they were still screaming, squirming, bawling, for the first time out of the dark, warm wetness, eyes not even open—now open but not focused, how do eyes focus? Focus is attention! What the hell is attention? How do you center on one thing and not another? Why is it so bright here? It's too full of color, of outline, of shadow, and too dense with sounds, rumbles, breaths, gasps, laughs, what in god's name is a laugh? How does the newly born see the world and then write it "as if for the first time, without the constant intimidation of being aware of what other writers have already done. In the mid-1960s that was exactly the feeling I had." So wrote Tom Wolfe in 1972 in *New York* Magazine, simultaneously experiencing, inventing, and chronicling what was called "new journalism," whose sometimes hyperventilating style this paragraph caricatures.

It began with reporters who wrote for magazines with literary pretensions like *Esquire* and for magazines with scarcely any pretensions at all, like the "Sunday supplement" magazines in daily newspapers, which is where *New York* began, as the Sunday supplement of the *New York Herald Tribune*. It had its heroes—like Gay Talese, Joan Didion, or Wolfe himself. They were reporters who were writing "features" for newspapers but who tried to publish as much as they could in the magazines that would take longer pieces. They were attracted to experiments with point-of-view and other literary devices. And they believed that in nonfiction, as long as it was genuinely reported observation, they could use any literary device "to excite the reader both intellectually and emotionally."

What made New Journalism "new" was literary freedom; what made it "journalism" was that it was reported. "New journalism" stood evenly for both. What struck critics of New Journalism as outrageous was the way the writers seemed to go inside the minds of the people they were writing about, even on occasion concocting an inner monologue (but only, Wolfe insists, with words the subject had actually uttered in the course of interview and observation). The value of New Journalism, Wolfe said, was to go beyond normal journalism to stay with the subject longer, to get the language, gestures, facial expressions, all the details, the stuff that in fiction gives readers such a vivid sense of the reality of characters who do not exist—only, in the new journalism, they did.

In retrospect, the impact of New Journalism was limited. It did little to make newspapers more literary—its location and its impact was primarily in magazine journalism. Newspapers and television barely noticed it, although many years later you can detect its influence in radio, notably National Public Radio's "This American Life." It encouraged some writers of fiction to try their hand at reporting—notably Norman Mailer and Truman Capote. And you can see versions of it in alternative media and in "Style" sections of the *New York Times*, *Washington Post*, and other papers. But perhaps the largest impact, one that can be detected among journalism students even today, is that it set a sparkle in the eye of aspiring reporters. Some young people still come to journalism to launch themselves as artists of society where they have a warrant—and press credentials—for seeing the world afresh and for turning it into vivid prose or documentary film and video or radio portraiture.

Did the press uncover the Watergate scandal? (And what was the Watergate scandal?)

Probably the most famous news reporting in all of American history and the most celebrated single bit of news reporting worldwide was the *Washington Post* investigation of the set of incidents we know as "Watergate." This reporting took place over an extended period from the summer of 1972 to the summer of 1974.

Watergate forced President Richard M. Nixon to resign from the Presidency, the only President ever to do so. Had he not resigned, he almost certainly would have been forced from office by impeachment. The House of Representatives had approved three articles of impeachment and the Senate was ready to serve as judge and jury as to whether he was guilty of the charges. Even Nixon's strong supporters in the Senate could count the votes and knew the Senate would vote to remove him from office.

Why? Because the evidence was convincing that Nixon had abused the powers of his office, using his position to mount attacks on those he considered his personal enemies—the press, the movement against the war in Vietnam, and the Democratic Party. Nixon approved plans of aides, sometimes initiating the plans himself, to burglarize the offices of Democratic candidates for President and also to burglarize Daniel Ellsberg's psychiatrist's office. Ellsberg was the Pentagon official who in 1971 had leaked "the Pentagon Papers" to the *New York Times*. The Nixon cabal hoped to find information they could leak to sully Ellsberg's reputation.

The "smoking gun" that led to Nixon's downfall was the tape-recorded evidence that proved the President ordered his aides to cover up burglaries and other petty, mischievous, but decidedly criminal activities he supported in his reelection campaign. This criminality included decisively the "obstruction of justice" that Nixon's own tape recordings revealed—Nixon's demanding that his aides instruct the C.I.A. to order the F.B.I. to call off its inquiries into the Watergate burglars, on the pretext that national security matters were at stake. For some analysts, this "cover-up" was worse than the original crimes, although reporters Carl Bernstein and Bob Woodward would later argue, to the contrary, that the crimes covered up were themselves "a brazen and daring assault, led by Nixon himself, against the heart of American democracy: the Constitution, our system of free elections, the rule of law."

When Bernstein and Woodward began their reporting of the original June 17, 1972, burglary of the Democratic National Committee headquarters in the Watergate office and condo complex in Washington, they had no idea what they were about to open up, nor did their editors at the *Washington Post*. Nor did others in the news media. Nixon may have considered the news media his enemies, but journalists considered Nixon an unusually smart, shrewd politician with a very safe shot at reelection; they found it just not credible that the White House was directly involved in burglaries (paying hush money to the burglars) and a long list of "dirty tricks" launched against different Democratic candidates. Why would a man so smart get involved with operations so dumb?

It took the rest of the press a long time to climb aboard the Watergate express. Meanwhile, much was revealed by non-media-related agencies of investigation—Federal Judge John Sirica pried information out of the arrested burglars; the Democratic National Committee and the private group Common Cause initiated lawsuits against the government that disclosed other relevant information; the Senate established a special "Watergate" committee to examine Watergate in a series of nationally televised hearings during the summer of 1973. As time passed, the biggest revealer of secrets was Richard Nixon himself, once it became known that he had secretly tape-recorded his many meetings in the Oval Office, leading federal prosecutors to subpoena the tapes.

No one doubts the importance of—and the courage of—the *Washington Post* in pursuing the investigation when few others were interested in it. Their efforts alone could not have pushed Nixon from office, but their dogged dedication to the story secured investigative reporting as the moral center of what is best in journalism.

What is the legacy of "the sixties" in journalism?

"New Journalism" influenced the daily production of news only around the edges, primarily in magazines. Investigative reporting that expanded during the Vietnam war years left a powerful legacy, but it is too expensive, risky, and time-consuming to color much of daily news production. Did the cultural upheavals of the 1960s contribute in the long term to the practice of everyday news reporting?

Yes, very much so. Changes can be seen in both the way news is written and in the attitudes and self-images of the journalists who produce it. The biggest change may be that the sixties created an enduring set of doubts that authority can be trusted. "Question Authority" was a popular slogan of the day, reproduced on buttons and T-Shirts—and also in the habits of mind and heart that became almost second-nature in journalism.

Journalists came to question the authority of government officials and other sources, and news stories in major daily newspapers grew longer and more analytical. Sources came to be more carefully and fully identified. Not only did reporters show a new skepticism of their sources, but they no longer also assumed their audiences would accept their own work without question. At the same time, the reporter's voice found a place more often—not so much a personal voice, a la New Journalism, but a voice of intellectual judgment. This was not the reporter's personal judgment but the reporter reflecting an attitude that politicians and other authorities are human, fallible, and self-interested, and that their statements are political actions rather than descriptions of reality. Reporters were not necessarily naïve about this earlier, but they were not reflective about the ways their own practices contributed to perpetuating the view that "the people in charge" basically knew what they were doing and wished only for the public good. In comparing ten daily papers from around the country from 1963 and 1999, a close observer of the news media was taken aback when he found in the 1963 papers that stories were "often not attributed at all, simply passing along an unquestioned, quasi-official sense of things. The world view seemed white, male, middle-aged, and middle class, a comfortable and confident Optimist Club bonhomie."

When Meg Greenfield, editorial page editor of the *Washington Post* in the 1980s and 1990s, recalled her early career in Washington journalism in the 1950s, she confessed—that's her term—that in those days she had taken it for granted that the people she covered were "basically honest, competent, and usually effective." Newsroom culture in the 1950s assumed that "the people in charge in Washington knew best."

After Vietnam, after Watergate, after the rising level of educational attainment in the population at large and among journalists in particular, after the "question authority" revolution that journalists identified with so strongly, newsroom insouciance in Washington and elsewhere faded. News grew more negative and more critical of political leaders; reporters asked more assertive and probing questions of presidents in news conferences; stories grew longer and offered context that quoted sources did not provide. They referred more to the past and to the future; they moved decisively from an emphasis on "who, what, when, where" to consideration of "why."

In a study that Katherine Fink and Michael Schudson conducted of three US newspapers from the 1950s to the early 2000s, the percentage of front-page stories judged "contextual" rather than "conventional" in the style of reporting increased (in all three papers) from under 10% to about 50% . The largest change came in the late 1960s and 1970s, but change continued in the same direction—toward more contextual reporting—at each measured point thereafter. A growing body of research converges in its portrayal of a shift toward increasingly vigorous and in some respects adversarial treatment of government officials, political candidates, and their policies.

The growth of contextual journalism represents a much larger quantitative change in news content than a reallocation of effort to investigative reporting. This had something to do with Vietnam. It had something to do with Watergate. But very similar findings appear in European journalism at the same time. Separate studies from Norway, Sweden, France, and Germany—of newspapers and of public broadcasting, too—all demonstrate a growing skeptical and critical edge in the same years. All show, as well, that reporters were more willing to intervene and interject in speaking to or speaking about politicians rather than simply hand over the responsibility for the communication to the political figures themselves.

So why the change? There is no simple answer, but we suspect that a growing prevalence of college education among journalists and a growing insistence on news professionalism had a lot to do with it. This was coupled with a new democratizing trend that took politicians (and doctors and lawyers and clergy and college professors) several steps down from their pedestals.

Question authority! Journalists came to believe that their field had a special public obligation to do exactly that.

Are the terms "contextual" or "analytical" or "explanatory" or "interpretive" news just euphemisms for biased news?

There is a difference between opinion that is shaped by evidence, even evidence inconvenient for the perspective the author would like to take—and opinion so set in stone that no accumulation of evidence can dislodge it. There is a difference between exploring a subject and preaching about it. In everyday life, we all know we cannot entirely escape our initial standpoint whether in terms of gender, race, and ethnicity, or height and weight. We see the world from our own vantage. At the same time, we also have experienced the honest effort to put our background to the side to try to see a situation from someone else's position. Someone may ask what to do regarding a dilemma or choice before them. We listen—that is the first task, and respond, "Well, if I were in your shoes . . . ," trying to imagine what would be the other person's—not our own—best interest. Can we ever do this fully? No. Can we take an honest stab at it? Certainly.

Much of the world's economic, political, military, diplomatic, social, and cultural currents are not easy to present simply. This does not mean that journalists should be confined to just presenting official reports and speeches and quoting leaders from the top parties and calling it a day. This practice, as critics began to say with growing insistence in the 1960s and 1970s, is itself a bias—a bias toward the established, the official, and the conventional. The reporter can and to some extent must think through, analyze, frame, and interpret—regardless of his or her own wishes about what the evidence *should* mean. The reporter's first question is what does the evidence *actually* mean?

Did people ever trust the press?

The short answer is "no." But that requires a little explaining, especially when people still often recall—incorrectly—that the long-time CBS News television anchor Walter Cronkite was in his day "the most trusted man in America." Cronkite, born in 1916, grew up in Kansas and Texas, and studied two years at the University of Texas before dropping out and working in journalism—wire services, a newspaper, radio, and, starting in 1950, television, working for CBS affiliates and moving up. In 1962, he became the CBS News anchor, the impresario of the network's flagship news program. He imprinted himself on American audiences—at least on the one-third or so of the audience that preferred CBS to its rivals ABC and NBC—and he remained the anchor until he retired in 1981. His coverage of the news of John F. Kennedy's assassination is celebrated, especially the tear in his eye and the lump in his throat as he announced Kennedy's death. His delight in the US space program is also well remembered.

But did this make him the most trusted man in America? A public opinion poll in 1972 asked respondents which of the leading political figures of the day they trusted most. Cronkite's name was thrown in apparently as a kind of standard of comparison—how do any and all of the politicians compare to some well-known and well-regarded nonpolitical figure? Seventy-three percent of those polled placed Cronkite first—followed by a general construct—"average senator"

(67%)—and Senator Edmund Muskie (61%). Chances are that any other leading news person—or probably many a movie star, athlete, or prominent scientist—would have come out as well or better than Cronkite. A 1974 poll found Cronkite less popular than rival TV news stars John Chancellor, Harry Reasoner, and Howard K. Smith. It appears that the main reason Cronkite was "most trusted" is simply that he was not a politician.

So the notion that Cronkite was unusually "trusted" is a phantom best forgotten. This does not mean that journalists have never been trusted, but it does mean that there is no basis to one of the most cited pieces of evidence that consensus and comity prevailed about the news media in the years 1945–1968 just before growing social upheaval around the Vietnam War and about civil rights erupted and spread.

The idea that the press had been a perfectly trusted pillar of mainstream, neutral, moderate, responsible news reporting is largely an illusion. Presidential candidate Adlai Stevenson ran in 1952 against what he called the "one-party press"—Republican—and of course he was right if you looked at the corporate ownership of the country's newspapers, their antagonism toward Franklin Roosevelt and the New Deal, and their overwhelming editorial-page support for Republicans. If you go back very much further than the 1940s, you reach a moment where "trust in the news media" is not even a sensible topic. The news media were understood to be and understood themselves to be advocates for one party or the other, not neutral truth-tellers. Readers trusted their own favored paper and distrusted the others.

Has Fox News ushered in the return of the partisan press?

Fox News began in 1996. It was not the first news outlet to revive partisanship. Credit for that must go to "talk radio," not news reporting but strictly news commentary, and far more often than not conservative in political views. This, and later partisan TV news programming, was made possible by the 1987 withdrawal of the "fairness doctrine," a Federal Communications Commission regulation that required broadcasters covering controversial issues to do so giving various viewpoints a hearing. When broadcasting—television especially—was a very limited resource, deregulators successfully argued, there may have been a need for the fairness doctrine, but no longer with the abundance of opportunities for speech in a cable television era.

The trend to partisanship in radio and cable TV is significant but it does not reproduce for the present anything like the partisan press that dominated American media in the nineteenth century. Fox (on the right) and MSNBC (on the left), while they have ardent followers, have equivocal influence. While research makes it clear that Fox viewers have more conservative opinions than non-Fox viewers, it is not clear whether conservative viewers seek out Fox or whether viewers from various political persuasions become more conservative because they watch Fox; the former is surely true, the latter is no doubt a part of the story but it may be a small part.

A partisan press in the nineteenth century when there was very little else, and a few partisan outlets in the wake of the development of strong professional, contextual journalism are very different things. Journalism schools, journalism awards, journalism values are all dominated by professional-style, not partisan-style, news. To the extent that Fox and MSNBC show themselves able to break important stories rather than to just spin in a partisan direction what other media have already reported, they may gain some ground—but this would be to put professional journalism and not partisanship in the driver's seat.

Moreover, television news for the most part follows print—that is, broadcast journalism still rarely breaks stories and rarely does investigative work of the sort that makes waves and sets new patterns. That is mostly the work of print or, today, print-plus-online news organizations, and especially those print outlets that for decades have led the way—the Associated Press, the *New York Times*, the *Wall Street Journal*, the *Washington Post*, and other leading newspapers that dominate a specific city, state, or region.

Even in television news, the cable channels, including Fox, have not equaled the audience size of CBS, NBC, or ABC, let alone the three of them together. That, of course, is if we compare the audience of the Fox News Channel evening news against the older networks' programs at that time slot, but Fox runs news programming around the clock. This makes it difficult to compare the audience sizes of all-news cable channels to the traditional entertainment-centered broadcast channels with limited hours for news. Still, many people who fear the influence of Fox because they do not share its conservative views, or do not approve its obviously partisan approach to news, exaggerate its place in the total array of television news programming.

The largest impact of cable television on the news audience, as media scholar Markus Prior has carefully argued, is not to poach viewers from the three major broadcast networks but to divert tens of millions of viewers from all TV news outlets toward sports channels, home shopping channels, movie channels, and other non-news programming. Many of the people least interested in national political news who once picked up a modicum of information from ABC, CBS, and NBC abandoned television news altogether for the array of more diverting cable channels.

2

THE PRESENT

What is news—and what is journalism—today?

News is everywhere today. It is on all kinds of mobile digital devices, on computer and television screens in homes and offices, on car radios, even in bus and airport waiting areas, and, still, on the printed page. News now comes from a myriad of sources around town and around the world: newspapers, television, radio and their websites, digital-only news and information sites and blogs, social media like Twitter and Facebook, e-mail, text messages, and shared photographs and videos, even Web search engines. News can now be produced by anyone with a digital phone, tablet, or laptop wherever they are—in addition to traditional news media with their printing presses, broadcast towers, satellite dishes, cable transmissions, Internet servers, and social media access.

It is news if it informs us—even with only a snippet of information or a single image—about something noteworthy, interesting, or relevant. In some ways, we decide for ourselves what news is now; it is no longer defined only by traditional news media. We can share news digitally without depending on the news media—or by picking and choosing what we consume and share from them. We can even participate in their newsgathering and commentary.

But news is not necessarily journalism, in which newsworthy information and comment is gathered, filtered, evaluated, edited, and presented in credible and engaging forms, whether writing, photography, video, or graphics. At its best, journalism puts news into context, investigates, verifies, analyzes, explains, and engages. It embodies news judgment oriented to the public interest.

It is now relatively easy for journalists to produce news on their own in individual blogs or videos on the Internet—just as lone journalists had long been able to do in printed books or newsletters. But something is still gained today when journalism can be pursued collectively in news organizations, large or small, with sufficient staff, support, and institutional authority to have greater impact, amplified by digital distribution. However their journalism is distributed and shared today, news organizations of various kinds still account for the lion's share of credible news about local, national, and international affairs, including investigative reporting that holds accountable governments and powerful private interests. Just over 60% of Americans still prefer to get news initially reported by those news organizations, whether in print, broadcast, or digital forms, according to a 2014 survey by the American Press Institute's Media Insight Project.

Many news organizations are now trying to evolve in the digital age into new shapes and journalistic missions, many of them overlapping. Newspaper newsrooms are producing websites with their own blogs and videos, often mixed with links to content from other news organizations, and are actively pursuing audiences for their news content on social media. Television and radio newsrooms are posting written versions of their news reporting and commentary on their websites. Digital startups are producing their own journalism and aggregating content from other media, contributors, and their own audiences. Some startup websites, which have amassed large digital audiences with celebrity gossip, games, trivia lists, and eye-catching photos and videos, are now also investing in news reporting. Other news sites specialize in investigative reporting, explaining the news, or focusing on niche subjects like government, politics, business, legal issues, technology, and sports. And increasing numbers of news organizations of all kinds are collaborating with each other across digital platforms and geographic boundaries to produce and disseminate more journalism than any of them could do alone.

But many news organizations—old and new—also are fighting to survive today. In ways we will explain, the financial foundations of traditional news media have yet to be rebuilt after the digital earthquake, while most digital startups have yet to prove that any of their various fledgling economic models are sustainable. Paradoxically, at a time when there is more news than ever before, and the best journalism may be better than ever, American journalism is in a state of great turmoil and uncertainty.

How has digital technology been changing the news—and journalism?

Whenever and wherever news breaks today, the first reports and images often arrive in newsrooms and on people's mobile devices via social media—whether transmitted by journalists or by ordinary citizens who happen to be at the scene of events. Journalists can sometimes initially reach witnesses and sources through those same social media. They can quickly search the Internet for background, context, and relevant records and data. They can use a steadily growing number of creative digital tools to organize, analyze, and display information.

As they piece a story together, working to verify, explain, and interpret its content, journalists and their news organizations can rapidly post what they are finding in social media messages, blog items, early versions of the story, and even photos and videos—sometimes attracting additional information from sources or readers reacting to what they have posted. They no longer have to wait for the next edition of a printed newspaper or the next scheduled television or radio broadcast. An increasing number of journalists with multimedia skills also can produce their own photographs and videos, and their news organizations can use digitally transmitted images from members of the public. Finished stories can be presented on websites and mobile devices in a variety of audience-engaging ways. And all of it can be distributed digitally far beyond the confines of print circulation and broadcast signals or national boundaries. News consumers can choose among many digital forms of journalism from an almost infinite variety of sources and share them through social media.

In these ways and more, digital technology is profoundly changing the news and journalism. It has enabled faster, broader, deeper, and more participatory news reporting that can be distributed digitally to potentially much larger audiences. It has made possible new, more informative, and engaging ways to present news by digitally integrating text, video, slide shows, animations, interactive charts, maps, and other graphics, and searchable databases with links to source materials. For example, readers of the digital presentation of the prize-winning 2013 *Milwaukee Journal Sentinel* stories about dangerous delays in required genetic screening of newborn babies in US hospitals were able to easily search an interactive map for what was happening in their states.

But digital technology also has destabilized news organizations that had long produced most of the news and set journalistic standards. Digital media have fragmented audiences and undermined the advertising-based economic models of once dominant newspapers and television and radio networks and stations. As the advertising revenue that had effectively subsidized news gathering continues to shrink steadily, many American news organizations have cut costs by drastically reducing their newsroom staffs and payrolls—and, in too many cases, by lowering their journalistic ambitions.

Today there are far fewer newspaper and television journalists covering everything from local and state to national and foreign news, in addition to subjects like education, the environment, health care, and science. The number of full-time newsroom employees at the nearly 1400 American daily newspapers, for example, has fallen from 54,100 in 2005 to just 32,900 in 2015, according to an annual survey by the American Society of Newspaper Editors. After several years of staff reductions, employment has stabilized somewhat in network and local television news, according to the Pew Research Journalism Project. But those journalists are spread more thinly over an increased number of hours of news at local stations and national cable networks. The number of news-gathering jobs shed by long-established news media still dwarfs the number created so far by digital startups, which account for only about 7% of the estimated 70,000 journalists now employed by American print, broadcast, and digital news media, according to the Pew Research Journalism Project's 2014 State of the News Media report.

At the same time, digital startups have kept multiplying, without the burden of the legacy costs of expensive printing presses, physical distribution, broadcast facilities, or transmission towers—and the employees to run them. Digital technology enables startup news websites to be more entrepreneurial and experimental as they seek both to fill gaps left by downsizing legacy media and to create new forms of journalism. Many have focused on local and state news and investigative reporting, a few others on foreign news. Some have involved their audiences more deeply in gathering and sharing news; others have specialized in new kinds of analytical, opinionated, or advocacy journalism, independent of corporate ownership and traditional journalistic standards. But many of the digital startups also are struggling to create sustainable economic models.

While disrupting old economic models, digital technology has created some new revenue opportunities for both new and old news media. Many are now requiring paid subscriptions for some or all of their digital news. To attract advertisers, they offer digital data about audience traffic and demographics. Many also are selling digital advertising that looks and reads much like news stories on the same websites and mobile applications, which makes it more difficult for you to distinguish news from digital ads. Some like Gannett newspapers and the Dallas Morning News have started digital marketing services for local businesses. Yet, for newspapers in particular, the new digital revenue so far has amounted to only a fraction of the pricier print advertising revenue they have lost.

Both new and old news media also are using digital technology to closely monitor the size and news habits of their audiences, including audiences for individual stories, images, and features on their websites. Some news organizations are using these audience metrics to evaluate the productivity of their journalists and the popularity of their stories, even basing compensation on that data. Some also are using digital traffic data to decide what news to cover, rather than relying only on journalists' news judgment.

Digital technology has made immediacy—being first with new or breaking news on social media, news sites, and search engines—an even more important factor in the competition for news audiences. And it is changing how journalists and newsrooms work. Posting news fast and first, often by minimizing or bypassing editorial review and fact-checking, can attract a larger digital audience.

At times, however, such haste can imperil accuracy and understanding, as we've seen with erroneous early reports of breaking news by both news media and citizens using social media. For example, several innocent young men were wrongly linked by television and social media reports to the 2012 Boston Marathon terrorist bombings. Later that year, Ryan Lanza was initially identified by cable television and digital media as the man who shot to death twenty children and six adults at a Newtown, Connecticut, elementary school, when the shooter was actually his brother, Adam, who also killed himself. The first cable television reports about the US Supreme Court's 2012 decision largely upholding the Affordable Care Act wrongly told everyone watching that the court had overturned the law because CNN and Fox News reporters had not yet read the entire complex ruling.

Digital technology also makes it easier for news-like rumors, half-truths, and purposeful misinformation to spread rapidly on the Internet before the truth catches up with them, if it ever does. For example, opinion polls have repeatedly shown that 10% or more Americans still doubt that President Obama was born in the United States, after years of false rumormongering by so-called "birthers," much of it on the Internet.

On the other hand, digital technology also gives news media and their audience new tools to correct mistakes, check facts, provide context, update information, reveal plagiarism and fabrication, and authenticate or discredit social media posts and citizen-contributed photos and videos. It enables anyone posting news on the Internet to include hyperlinks to primary source material and other relevant information and images. It gives news media the means to show how they cover the news and what goes into their journalism, and it gives their audience opportunities to help shape the news. The same technology that has so disrupted American journalism is enabling its reconstruction in still evolving new forms.

What has not changed—and what should not change?

News still plays a significant role in many of our lives, our communities and our world. What was written in *The News About the News* at the dawn of the digital transformation of news at the turn of the century in the United States (Leonard Downie Jr. and Robert G. Kaiser, Knopf, 2002, p.6), is still relevant today:

> Good journalism—in a newspaper or magazine, on television, radio, or the Internet—enriches Americans by giving them both useful information for their daily lives and a sense of participation in the wider world. Good journalism makes possible the cooperation among citizens that is critical to a civilized society. Citizens cannot function together as a community unless they share a common body of information about their surroundings, their neighbors, their government bodies, their sports

> teams, even their weather. Those are all the stuff of news. The best journalism digs into it, make sense of it and makes it accessible to everyone.

Good journalism bears witness and describes, engages and informs, verifies and explains, analyzes and interprets, creates understanding and empathy, investigates and reveals—and, most importantly, seeks after truth. Whatever form it takes and however it is produced in the digital age, good journalism has not changed in these fundamental ways.

Bad journalism—reporting news inaccurately, inadequately, unfairly, or mendaciously—also has not fundamentally changed, although its impact tends to be magnified by the long reach of digital media.

So news values still matter. In a turbulent sea of too often untrustworthy digital information, news values are the beacons for credible journalism. *We believe that vital news values* include accuracy, fairness, open-mindedness, independence of power and ideology, transparency about sources and methods whenever possible, and dedication to accountability and the public interest. Every news organization and everyone producing news on their own should embody these news values, even, as we will discuss, when news takes the form of analysis, commentary, or advocacy.

It is not always easy. Many news organizations have had to discipline—and, when necessary, fire—journalists who were careless with facts or fabricated information, demonstrated blatant bias, plagiarized, or engaged in other kinds of unprofessional conduct that undermine a news organization's credibility.

With even the best of intentions, digital competition for speed can threaten accuracy. Advocacy can trump fairness. Pressure from news media owners or intimidating outside influences can compromise independence. The identities of some sources may need to be shielded to protect their livelihoods or even their lives. Fairness, open-mindedness, accountability, and the public interest, as we will explore, can be variously defined, and there can be legitimate disagreement about just what these values mean and how they can best be realized in practice. But accuracy—the pursuit of truth—should be an unambiguous objective, even when it can only be painstakingly pursued a step at a time.

"Journalism's first obligation is to the truth," Bill Kovach and Tom Rosenstiel emphasized in their essential book about the news, *The Elements of Journalism*. "Even in a world of expanding voices, 'getting it right' is the foundation upon which everything else is built—context, interpretation, comment, criticism, analysis, and debate. The larger truth, over time, emerges from this forum."

Who pays for the news these days?

News is expensive. Yes, countless fragments of sometimes newsy information can be shared for free on the Internet today. And anyone can report or share an image on social media of something they've just heard or seen—or post it on any of the myriad blogs for which there is no compensation. But trained journalists and the staff and infrastructure of credible news organizations are expensive, regardless of technology. Before the digital revolution, advertising paid for most news in the United States, in print or broadcasting, supplemented in print by the relative pittance that readers paid for their newspapers, which did not even cover the cost of the ink and paper. But advertising, along with news audiences, has been fragmented by digital and cable television alternatives. The nearly 1400 daily newspapers in the United States in particular have lost more than half of their advertising revenue in just a decade—falling from $46 billion in 2003 to an estimated $20.7 billion in 2013, according to the Newspaper Association of America. Classified advertising for everything from cars and jobs to homes for sale and rent made up the largest share of that decline, according to Poynter Institute media business analyst Rick Edmunds, plummeting from just over $15 billion in 2003 to just over $4 billion in 2013, thanks to popular digital alternatives.

As a result, there have been dramatic changes in who pays for the news.

Newspapers, for example, are now charging their less numerous print readers significantly more for individual copies of and subscriptions to their printed papers. A majority of newspapers, including most of the largest in readership, also are charging digital readers for access to their websites and mobile applications. Many set up so-called metered paywalls, which allow visitors to view a certain number of stories—on most newspaper sites five to twelve per month—before they are required to pay to subscribe. Others require a paid subscription for any access. Altogether, newspaper income from print and digital paid subscriptions reached $10.9 billion in 2013, according to the Newspaper Association of America, accounting for nearly 30% of newspapers' total revenue, compared to just 16% in 2007.

Some newspapers and digital news sites also are offering access to journalists and newsmakers at various kinds of special events for premium payments. Others, such as *The Wall Street Journal, Chicago Tribune,* and *Los Angeles Times*, have bundled print and digital subscriptions, access to other content, special events, and even entertainment discounts into monthly paid memberships. However, even as audience revenue has been, on balance, increasing in these ways, steadily declining advertising still accounts for two-thirds of the revenue for all of American journalism, including print, broadcast, and digital, according to a 2014 Pew Research Journalism Project study.

Newspapers, although still mostly profitable after severe cost-cutting, are nevertheless seen as relatively unattractive long-term investments in their current forms. Many longtime corporate owners of large groups of newspapers and television stations—including Gannett, Tribune, Scripps, and Rupert Murdoch's News Corp.—have divested their newspaper holdings into separate companies, away from somewhat more profitable television stations and other assets. Still other newspaper owners, including investment companies speculating in media acquisitions, have offered their stripped-down newspapers for sale outright, with their fates unknown.

But, among the recent buyers of selected newspapers at bargain prices are billionaires with agendas. Investor Warren Buffett added twenty-eight papers in small and medium-sized cities in 2011, 2012, and 2013 to the forty-one he already owned. Amazon founder Jeff Bezos purchased *The Washington Post* in 2013. In the same year, Boston Red Sox (baseball) owner and former hedge fund executive John Henry took *The Boston Globe* off the hands of *The New York Times*, and Minnesota Timberwolves (basketball) owner Glen Taylor, bought *The Star-Tribune* in Minneapolis-St. Paul.

Henry and Taylor said they want to help *The Globe* and *The Star-Tribune* survive as vital local newspapers. "I see The Boston Globe and all that it represents as another great Boston institution that is worth fighting for," Henry told the newspaper's readers. Bezos said he wants *The Washington Post* to prosper as a digitally enhanced local, national, and international multimedia news organization. "For me," he told *Post* journalists at a newsroom meeting, "it's an exciting opportunity to participate in something that's a pillar of a free society."

"I believe that papers delivering comprehensive and reliable information to tightly-bound communities and having a sensible Internet strategy will remain viable for a long time," financier Buffett wrote about his strategy of buying newspapers that still have relatively substantial local audiences and advertising support. "Wherever there is a pervasive sense of community, a paper that serves the special information needs of that community will remain indispensable to a significant proportion of its residents."

In another sign of the changing times, Alice Rogoff, daughter of a wealthy digital innovator and wife of Carlyle Group billionaire investor David Rubenstein, bought the *Alaska Dispatch* digital news site in 2009, and then the *Anchorage Daily News* newspaper in 2014. She created the print and digital

Alaska Dispatch News, now by far the state's dominant news organization.

Local newspaper ownership by wealthy individuals is an old American tradition. Their patronage can protect news organizations somewhat from the whims of the marketplace, but it can also raise news coverage and conflict of interest questions. All the wealthy new newspaper owners have pledged not to interfere with newsgathering. But it's likely that people will be watching to see how *The Post* covers Bezos and Amazon, how the *Star-Tribune* and the *Globe* cover the Timberwolves and the Red Sox and their owners' other holdings, and how the *Alaska Dispatch News* covers the Carlyle Group's extensive investments in Alaska.

The ownership of television stations that broadcast local news is mostly concentrated in large corporations, including the major networks and companies like Sinclair Broadcast Group, which owns and operates more than 160 television stations reaching almost 40% of the US population. Some of their owner relationships also raise coverage questions. Local station owners ABC (The Walt Disney Company), CBS (Sumner Redstone's National Amusements), NBC (Comcast's NBC Universal), and Fox (Rupert Murdoch's 20th Century Fox) are controlled by high-profile entertainment companies with products to be promoted and images to protect, while Sinclair uses its stations to spread its aggressive conservative ideology.

Television station advertising, although not as robust in recent years as in the past, plus the retransmission fees that stations charge cable companies to carry their channels, make them still comparatively profitable. News programs and websites account for almost half the revenue of the average television station, according to the Radio Television Digital News Association, because there is more local advertising time for each station to sell during local newscasts than during network and syndicated shows.

In the digital world, media entrepreneurs have started popular and diverse for-profit websites like BuzzFeed, Gawker,

Vice, Vox, Politico, and TMZ, which are producing digital news in a variety of forms, along with blogs, gossip, pop culture, video programs, and entertainment. They are competing with older digital aggregators of news content like Yahoo News, AOL News, and The Huffington Post, which also have been investing in original journalism. These digital operations, which have been luring experienced journalists away from traditional news organizations, are experimenting with new kinds of visual, explanatory, revelatory, and opinion journalism about everything from politics, national security, and foreign affairs to sports, lifestyles, and entertainment. Their revenue comes from varying combinations of advertising, digital subscriptions, and Internet marketing and consulting services. Some, such as BuzzFeed and Vice, also have attracted significant funding from venture capitalists, which, at least indirectly, injects new money into paying for news.

At the same time, foundations, universities, philanthropists, and other donors are funding a growing number of start-up nonprofit news organizations that are influencing American journalism beyond their still relatively small sizes and numbers. Some of the nonprofits like the Voice of San Diego focus on local news; others like Texas Tribune on state issues and still others like ProPublica on journalism of national interest. Some, such as Arizona State University's Cronkite News, which reports on Arizona for news media throughout the state, are based at universities and staffed by student journalists under professional supervision. Others are the expanded newsrooms of public radio stations like St. Louis Public Radio and New York Public Radio, which have been increasing their local and regional news coverage. Significantly, as we will explore later, many of the nonprofits collaborate with each other and with newspapers and television stations and networks so their journalism can reach wider audiences.

However, the finances of many of these fledgling nonprofit news organization are fragile at best. They depend on unpredictable grants from national and local foundations, private donations, audience memberships, and fundraising events. A few earn revenue from sharing the journalism and data they produce with other news media. Others are supported by universities so their students can do journalism while they are studying it. A fraction of the support for public radio stations that cover news—about 10% or so for most stations—is federal government money that passes through the independent Corporation for Public Broadcasting. Qualifying nonprofits also benefit from federal tax exemptions and tax-deductible donations from supporters, although Internal Revenue Service approval of the needed 501(c) (3) tax code designation for news nonprofits has been unpredictable in recent years.

Altogether, however, the various kinds of new money paying for digital news and innovations in journalism have not come close to filling the gap left by still shrinking advertising support. As the Pew Research Center's State of the News Media 2014 report concluded, "So far, the impact of new money flowing into the (news) industry may be more about fostering new ways of reporting and reaching audiences than about building a new, sustainable revenue structure."

Are newspapers dead? Or are some no longer newspapers?

There are still almost 1400 daily printed newspapers in the United States. Only a few have actually died in recent years—and the biggest casualties were the second newspapers in what had been two-newspaper cities, including Denver, Seattle, and Tucson. But scores of daily papers have stopped publishing on one or more days each week to save printing and delivery costs on days when they sell the least advertising. These include the *Times-Picayune* in New Orleans, *Birmingham News*, *Press-Register* of Mobile, and *Huntsville Times*—all owned by Advance Publications—which now publish papers only three days a week, posting news on their websites the rest of each week. Two other Advance papers, *The Oregonian* in Portland and *Plain Dealer* in Cleveland, publish and deliver home editions four days a week, putting smaller editions on newsstands the other days. The Advance newspapers' journalists now put all of their news on their websites, while small separate editorial staffs select some of it to be published in their print editions. The jointly operated *Detroit Free Press* and the *Detroit News* follow a similar pattern, having reduced home delivery of printed papers to just three days a week.

In addition to losing half their advertising revenue and cutting their newsroom staffs by 40% in the decade between 2005 and 2015, newspapers lost half of their print circulation during that time. Even with the addition of digital subscriptions in recent years, average paid daily circulation for US newspapers fell from 54.6 million in 2004 to 29.1 million in 2014, according to authoritative news media analyst Alan Mutter. At the same time, unpaid digital exposure of their news content in a variety of ways has actually increased audiences for newspaper-produced journalism, even though much of that is sporadic viewing via links from other websites and social media. Eight of every ten adults online in August 2014 viewed at least some newspaper digital content, according to comScore digital data released by the Newspaper Association of America (NAA). A 2014 Scarborough Research study for the NAA shows that 55% of the total audience for newspaper journalism still read it in print, 30% both in print and on digital devices, and 15% only on digital devices.

Many newspaper owners have focused on cutting costs to remain at least marginally profitable by further shrinking their news staffs and reducing pay—which has significantly degraded the quantity and quality of their news coverage—and eliminating days of print publishing while doing little more digitally than posting their content on websites. Many others are claiming to be converting themselves into "digital first" news organizations, but these initiatives sometimes appear to be primarily cost-cutting in digital dress. Only a relatively small number so far are investing in more ambitious transformations from traditional newspapers into innovative digital news organizations.

In 2015, Gannett, the largest US newspaper publisher as measured by paid circulation, spun off its then eighty-two newspapers, including *USA Today*, into a separate company from its forty-three television stations. It also made the latest in a series of deep news staff and salary cuts and directed many of its newspapers to become "newsrooms of the future," in which editors would be eliminated or repurposed, reporters would post unedited stories directly online, and much of what they cover would be dictated by what audience metrics show that readers prefer on their websites.

Journalists at the Gannett newspapers were instructed to reapply for fewer jobs. For example, at Gannett's *Indianapolis Star*, which employed 275 journalists in 2000, the 124 remaining staff members were told to compete for 106 jobs in 2014. "Every job has been redefined," Kate Marymount, Gannett's vice president for news, told the Columbia Journalism Review. "That's why everyone applies for a new job. There are some smaller number of jobs, so not everyone will find a job."

Amalie Nash, editor and vice president for audience engagement at Gannett's *Des Moines Register* in Iowa, told the Columbia Journalism Review that she was reducing the number of newsroom "middle managers," including traditional assignment editors. "Instead you have content strategists and coaches who work with teams of reporters on what they're covering," she said, "how to reach certain audiences, how to respond to what they're hearing through metrics and feedback and everything else."

After most local Gannett newspapers drastically deemphasized or eliminated national and foreign news, *USA Today* began in 2014 to insert a daily summary section of its national, international, financial, and lifestyle news into Gannett newspapers and their websites. Larry Kramer, who was then publisher of *USA Today*, said this enabled local Gannett papers to devote more resources to local news. It also increased *USA*

Today's print and digital audience, the largest in the country, for marketing to advertisers.

Advance Publications, privately owned by the Newhouse family, has gone further and re-oriented its thirty-three newspapers in eleven states to feed twelve local and regional news websites designed to be "new digitally focused news and information companies." Home delivery of the printed newspapers was eliminated several days a week to "free up millions of dollars to invest in our digital operations," according to an internal 2013 progress report memo from Randy Siegel, president of Advance Local. Newsroom staffs were cut drastically, some by well over half, leaving Advance journalists to work collectively in places like Alabama, where its news operations at the Birmingham, Huntsville, and Mobile newspapers were effectively subsumed into its Al.com digital site. As at many other newspapers across the country, Advance journalists are encouraged to help increase traffic on its websites by frequently posting breaking news, updates, blogs, photos, and responses to reader comments on the Advance websites, in addition to using social media to draw attention to their work.

The rhythms of newspaper newsrooms are now dictated by peak audience periods on the Internet—early morning, lunchtime, and just after school and work in many places—rather than the traditional evening deadlines for morning papers. Journalists working overnight may have deadlines around dawn. Others may face multiple deadlines—late morning and late afternoon, for example—for different digital and then print versions of developing stories. The smaller number of editors in most newsrooms handles both digital and print content. New jobs have been created for social media engagement, maximization of web traffic, creation of innovative blogs, and other digital journalism, and the production of videos, audio podcasts, and video news shows for the newspapers' websites.

Although there are many similarities in the ways various newsrooms are trying to transform themselves from traditional newspapers into multiplatform digital news organizations, there are not yet proven models, as there were in the newspapers' advertising-subsidized print past. So far, there are differences in the mix of print and digital audiences and revenue, in the speed and kinds of digital innovation, and in the amounts of new investments, if any. In particular, *The Washington Post* and *The New York Times,* with large national audiences, have drawn considerable attention for their approaches to digital transformation.

At *The Post,* Jeff Bezos injected new money and ambition into digital change that had begun before he bought the newspaper in 2013 from the public company (now Graham Holdings) controlled by Donald Graham and his family. In 2014, *The Post* hired more than one hundred people in its newsroom, reversing a long period of steady contraction. It opened software and audience development labs in New York and further integrated web developers with editors and reporters in its Washington newsroom to help develop a steady stream of innovative digital journalism for a fast-growing worldwide audience. Half of the fifty million unique visitors to *The Post*'s digital sites in July 2015 came from tablets and smartphones, much of that through web searches and social media links. *The Post*'s Newspaper Partner Program gave its digital national and international news to subscribers of the paid websites of more than 250 US daily newspapers, reaching an additional tens of thousands of digitally identifiable consumers of *The Post*'s journalism.

The New York Times refocused its newsroom on digital transformation in 2014, after The New York Times Company decided to concentrate its resources on the newspaper and its digital sites, selling off the *Boston Globe*, a group of regional newspapers, and other holdings. *The Times* had already established one of the first and most successful digital news paywalls, with one million paid digital subscribers in 2015. *The Times* commissioned a 96-page report in 2014 from a newsroom committee that noted "traditional competitors like *The Wall Street Journal, The Washington Post, The Financial*

Times, and *The Guardian* are moving aggressively to remake themselves as digital first—digital reports that also produce newspapers, rather than the other way around." In response to the report's recommendations, *The Times* reorganized its newsroom leadership to add senior editors in charge of digital strategy, interactive news technology, and audience development, plus new digital editors in all of its nine news departments.

Nearly half of the 70,000 journalists working at American news organizations are still in the newsrooms of newspapers and their digital operations. And those newsrooms, despite all their contraction and digital challenges, still originate much of the news that Americans see in print, on the Internet, and even on television. Should they still be called newspapers? They still publish some of their news in print. They still deliver it to some homes on paper, if not every day everywhere. Half of people who read news read it on paper only and another 30% read it both on paper and online. On the other hand, practically all firms that publish news on paper also publish online, though some do so more vigorously than others, seeing their websites as a creative opportunity for better reporting. They are becoming multimedia, multiplatform news organizations whose shapes are still evolving. Newspapers? Newspapers on the road to multimedia news organizations.

What's happened to news on television?

Television remains the most popular source of news for Americans, even as a majority of us also regularly consume news from newspapers, radio, and the Internet. A 2014 study by the American Press Institute's Media Insight Project found that 93% of Americans get at least some of their news from television stations, networks, and their websites; 66% from newspapers and their websites; 56% from radio stations and their websites; and 47% from digital-only sites like Yahoo! News and BuzzFeed.

There are now more hours of news on television than ever, even though the size of the news staffs of local stations and national networks has mostly stagnated after years of reductions to maintain their profitability. The content of both national network and local station television news appears to be primarily shaped by what is currently popular, with minute-to-minute measurements of audience ratings. News on television is characterized today by weather, traffic, crime, sports, and broadcasters' banter on expanded hours of local television news; celebrity interviews, lifestyle news, entertainment and more banter on the networks' long morning shows; disaster and lifestyle news along with digests of national and world developments on the networks' relatively brief evening newscasts; and endless hours of often opinionated talk on cable news.

After decades of decline, the combined audience for the flagship ABC, CBS, and NBC evening newscasts has steadied in recent years at a nightly average of about twenty-four million people in 2015. That is still much larger than the combined prime-time cable news audience of less than three million for CNN, Fox News, and MSNBC in 2014, according to the Pew Research Center and Nielsen Media Research. But news took up only 18.8 minutes of the broadcast networks' thirty-minute evening newscasts in 2012, according to a Pew study, with the rest of the time devoted to commercials and network promotions. Despite its name, ABC World News offered the least foreign news but the most crime, lifestyle, and entertainment news. NBC Nightly News aired somewhat more government and politics news, along with a sizeable amount of lifestyle news. CBS Evening News had notably less lifestyle news and the most foreign and national security news, even though CBS operated fewer overseas news bureaus, only five, after closing nine bureaus around the world between 2008 and 2012.

Since the Pew study, the three networks have further sped up the pace of their evening news programs—with ABC adding garish cable news-style graphics and melodramatic music and sound effects—and have devoted still more of each program's eighteen-plus minutes to audience-attracting human interest stories and Internet videos of odd occurrences, children, and animals. The changes likely are aimed at attracting younger viewers. Pew Research Center news media studies have repeatedly shown that the evening news audiences skew several years or more older than the median age for the US population of about 46.

News has been mostly marginalized on what had been the broadcast networks' other news shows. Their featured morning shows—ABC's *Good Morning America*, NBC's *Today*, and CBS's *This Morning*—have increasingly supplanted serious news coverage for their combined audience of twelve to thirteen million viewers with human interest features, entertainment, and talk, especially after their first half-hour on the air. With the exception of *60 Minutes* on CBS, with a consistent audience of eleven to twelve million on Sunday evenings, what had been in-depth prime-time news magazines—*Dateline* on NBC, *48 Hours* on CBS, and *20-20* and *Primetime* on ABC—have become tabloid television programs. They have featured melodramatic narratives of crimes, court cases, and bizarre occurrences, even as their audiences have fallen in the past decade to about five million viewers each.

All three broadcast networks have reduced their news staffs in recent years to cut costs, as estimated by Pew. They do not break out annual budget or staffing details for their news divisions. "Assessing the state of network newsrooms is difficult," Pew reported in 2011, "but available information suggests these newsrooms are less than half the size they were in the 1980s." With smaller news staffs, the broadcast networks are using more reporting and video from their local stations and other sources, including YouTube, Twitter, and other social media.

The Spanish-language Univision and Telemundo television networks, which feature telenovela soap operas and variety shows, also produce national news programs on weeknights that resemble those of the three major English-language networks and draw sizeable audiences.

The total audience for the three major cable news networks—CNN, Fox News, and MSNBC—has fallen in recent years to less than three million viewers in primetime and two million during the day, according to 2014 Pew and Nielsen data. But they reported in 2013 that cable news network consumers spend twice as much time watching each day as did viewers of broadcast network news. What those cable news viewers see today is more talk—interviews, commentary, and opinion—and less live coverage of breaking news and events, which had once distinguished cable news.

A Pew Research study of cable news content in 2012 showed that "overall, commentary and opinion are more prevalent throughout the day (63% of the airtime) than straight news reporting (37%)." Only CNN, which has a larger reporting staff and more news bureaus worldwide than any of the other broadcast or cable networks, has recently reversed that trend and increased its breaking news coverage, including from CNN International. Overall, CNN still broadcasts the most news of the three major cable news networks, according to Pew, while MSNBC did the least. MSNBC specialized in left-leaning political commentary and opinion. Fox News, which had a larger audience, featured right-leaning news coverage, commentary, and opinion, including a 2014 prime-time lineup of notably outspoken conservative commentators Bill O'Reilly, Greta Van Susteren, Sean Hannity, and Megyn Kelly.

Other ideologically oriented cable and satellite channels aimed at viewers on the political left or right have come and gone in recent years with none yet taking hold. One of them, Current TV, launched by former Vice President Al Gore, sold its channel space on American cable providers to the Al Jazeera Media Network, owned by the ruling family of Qatar. In 2013, it started short-lived Al Jazeera America, which offered national and international news produced by US journalists until closing down in 2016.

Besides the major general news and Spanish-language cable networks, there are a growing number of special interest channels, including CNBC, Fox Business Network, and Bloomberg TV for financial news; ESPN and other offshoots of the major broadcast networks for sports; and the Weather Channel.

Relatively little news appears on national public television in the United States. The non-profit Public Broadcasting Service (PBS), which has more than 350 member public television stations, does not produce news or any other programming. Instead, PBS acquires and distributes programs from large public stations, independent producers, and other sources, including Britain's BBC. Among those are a variety of documentaries, including Frontline investigations, NOVA science and technology programs, and American Experience history and biography films—all produced by public television station WGBH in Boston. The only daily news program on PBS is the struggling evening *News Hour*, formerly the *MacNeil-Lehrer News Hour*, which Robert MacNeil and Jim Lehrer donated to the Washington, DC public television station WETA in 2014. Its reported audience has plummeted from 2.5 million viewers in 2005 to less than one million in 2013, and it has lost millions in corporate donations to support what had been an annual budget of about $25 million.

Why does so much local television news look the same?

Local television news in the United States is formulaic—formatted by industry consultants to maximize audience ratings and advertising revenue. So it offers viewers look-alike news formats, most of which focus on presentation rather than substance. For "Eyewitness News," television reporters present their stories in live "stand-ups" in front of where a news event occurred earlier, even though the traffic accident had long ago been cleared from the intersection, or the courthouse where the trial took place is dark and empty. "Action News" contains fast-paced short stories and snippets of video, without much substantive reporting, to avoid losing impatient viewers. Local news programs with widely copied slogans like "On Your Side" or "Coverage You Can Count On" feature subjects like health and consumer news or crime fighting that can be promoted to viewers as having an impact on their lives.

During "sweeps" periods each February, May, July, and November, private "ratings" services measure audience size to establish a basis for setting advertising rates. During "sweeps" weeks, most stations showcase sensationalized crime, consumer, and investigative reporting in their news programs. Local stations also tend to reflect the branding and personalities of the networks with which they are affiliated. Industry insiders point out, for example, that ABC's network programming attracts more women viewers than CBS or NBC, so some ABC affiliates favor news stories they believe would appeal to women.

Weather, traffic, sports, crime, and unusual events dominate local commercial television newscasts. Pew Research Center studies of selected local stations' newscasts showed that the average time they devoted to weather, traffic, and sports increased from 32% in 2005 to 40% in late 2012 and early 2013. Coverage of what Pew characterized as "accidents, disasters, and unusual events" jumped from 5% of local news airtime in 2005 to 13% in late 2012–2013, in addition to the 17% of newscast time devoted to crime stories.

No doubt that weather and traffic reports are important public services and that sports news not only draws viewers but helps build a sense of local community. Still, coverage of local government and politics decreased from an already paltry 7% of air time in 2005 to only 3% in 2012–2013. "For some time, television consultants have been advising local television stations that viewers aren't interested in politics and government," Pew stated in its 2013 State of the News Media report, "and it appears that advice is being taken."

Local television newscasts often contain eye-catching video of weather events, disasters, crimes, and bizarre behavior that they obtain cheaply from stations and networks around the country and the world, as well as from social media and their own viewers. These video snippets are featured in newscasts even when they have no connection to the station's community. Many local stations also devote time in their newscasts to features about and promotions of programs on their affiliated networks, in addition to frequent promotions of the stations' own on-air anchors and reporters.

Even though audiences for local television news had been steadily declining overall until leveling off recently, stations have been adding newscasts, particularly in the early morning, so they can sell more local advertising. The average amount of time devoted to local station newscasts each weekday increased from 3.7 hours in 2003 to 5.4 hours in 2012, according to Pew.

But most stations have not increased their news staffs, which are much smaller than even shrunken newspaper staffs in most of the same cities. So the stations have increased time slots for advertising revenue on their newscasts without increasing their newsgathering costs. With their news staffs spread ever more thinly, the stations are even less likely to do in-depth reporting about their communities, virtually ignoring subjects like education, the environment, local business, and technology that are not believed to appeal to their audiences.

Spanish-language stations owned by Univision and NBC Universal's Telemundo also have increased their hours of local news, which resembles that of English-language stations and draws similar-sized audiences in cities like Los Angeles, Miami, and New York, with large Latino populations.

Some local stations have increased local investigative reporting, although much of it is little more than "watchdog" consumer stories, after television consultants' research showed that viewers want it and stations can build some of their branding around it. Station group owners such as NBC, Gannett, Hearst, and Scripps have encouraged the hiring and training of additional reporters and producers for their stations' investigative units, with many of the resulting stories aimed at sweeps weeks.

Most significantly, in many places around the country, the local television newscast looks exactly the same on two or more local stations because, in fact, it *is* the same. More than one-fourth—or 307—of the 1,026 American television stations that broadcast local news have been getting much or all of that news from another local station, according to a 2014 research report by Hofstra University Professor Bob Papper for the Radio Television Digital News Association. This is a result of steadily increasing consolidation in the ownership of local television stations. The largest station owners, as of 2014 according to Pew, are Sinclair Broadcast Group, which owns or operates 167 stations in seventy-seven local television markets, Gray Television with 124 stations in forty markets, Nexstar Broadcasting with 108 stations in forty-four markets, LIN Media with forty-three stations in twenty-three markets, Tribune with forty-two stations in thirty-four markets, Gannett Broadcasting with forty-three stations in thirty-three markets, Media General with thirty-one stations in twenty-eight markets, and CBS with twenty-nine stations in nineteen markets.

In many cities and towns, these companies own or operate two stations—called "duopolies"—and save money by closing the newsroom at one station, which then broadcasts the news produced by the other station, with the same on-air anchors and identical stories. In Eugene, Oregon, for example, the newsroom of KMTR, an NBC affiliate operated by Sinclair, was merged into the newsroom of KVAL, a CBS affiliate owned by Sinclair, and the two stations broadcast the same newscasts. In this way, these duopoly stations preserve their local newscast advertising time at much lower cost.

A 2013 Pew survey found that a growing number of stations with different owners also broadcast the same local news to save money. In Lansing, Michigan, for example, WLAJ, an ABC affiliate owned by Shield Media, simulcasts the newscasts produced by WLNS, a CBS affiliate owned by Media General. In Syracuse, New York, the combined newsroom of two separately owned stations affiliated with CBS and NBC produces identical local news stories for the stations' separately branded newscasts.

Greater quantities of local news can be found on 24-hour regional news channels operated by big media companies on cable television systems in some parts of the country. The seven largest are Time Warner Cable's NY1 and Cablevision's News12 Long Island in the New York City metropolitan area; Sinclair's News Channel 8 in the Washington, DC metropolitan area; Comcast's New England Cable News; Tribune's Chicagoland Television; Bright House Networks' Bay News 9 in the Tampa Bay area in Florida; and Gannett's Northwest Cable News in the states of Washington, Oregon, and Idaho.

These regional cable channels broadcast news around the clock in rotating blocks of live and repeated news and discussion shows, plus bulletins of updated news, weather, and sports. They augment their own news resources with content-sharing agreements with broadcast stations and newspapers in their areas, some of which have the same owners. For example, the Chicago Tribune newspaper and Tribune's WGN television station share content with Tribune's Chicagoland Television cable news channel. Gannett's television stations in Seattle, Portland, and Boise share video with its Northwest Cable News. These kinds of content sharing give viewers of regional cable news channels a greater volume of local news, if not the resources for deeper enterprise or investigative reporting. As subscription cable operations, their freedom from the pressures of audience ratings enables them to devote more news coverage and discussion programs to subjects like government, politics, business, education, technology, and culture, which are scarce on local broadcast television newscasts.

Meanwhile, most nonprofit public television stations do not produce or broadcast local news programs at all. PBS and station officials cite the high cost of televised newscasts, a lack of philanthropic support for news programming, a perceived lack of viewer interest, and competition with commercial television stations. Relatively few more ambitious public television stations are working with universities and other news organizations to produce their own local news. In a notable but rare example, San Diego's public television station, KPBS, operated by San Diego State University, broadcasts its own evening newscasts, with assistance on breaking news and video content from the local ABC-affiliated commercial station, 10 News San Diego. The KPBS public television station shares a sizeable newsroom with the KPBS public radio station, which also broadcasts local newscasts, and with inewsource.org, an independent startup nonprofit digital investigative news site in San Diego that works with KPBS radio and television on investigative projects. KPBS also shares a local news reporter with the Voice of San Diego nonprofit news site and collaborates with El Latino, San Diego's Hispanic newspaper, which publishes KPBS stories in Spanish. And KPBS produces its own digital news site.

How is digital technology changing television news?

Of course, digital technology—from satellite transmission to computerized graphics to miniaturization of video cameras—has long had a profound impact on television news. What is different with the Internet today is that digital technology is challenging television news rather than just enabling its broadcasting. The digital revolution is forcing networks and stations to evolve from traditional television to digital multimedia on many kinds of screens and devices.

The free-access digital news sites of the major broadcast and cable networks, for example, now attract much larger and younger audiences than their televised news programs. Their websites contain more news than their television newscasts, including print versions of news stories and streaming video and photo galleries that digital audiences can read and watch whenever they want. Yet the networks' websites produce only a small fraction of the advertising revenue of their television newscasts.

The websites of all of the major broadcast and cable news networks, which also contain content from other sources, are among the twenty most visited news sites in the United States, along with the digital versions of *The New York Times, The Washington Post* and *USA Today* newspapers, and digital-only sites like The Huffington Post and Google News. ABC and Yahoo formed a digital content partnership in 2012 that has drawn the Internet's largest news website audience, overtaking cnn.com. The majority of the audience for all these sites on which most digital visitors spend only a few minutes each day now comes from smartphones, tablets, and other mobile devices.

Local television stations have moved more slowly than the networks in evolving their websites from primarily promotional arms of the stations into comprehensive local news sites—and more slowly than many newspapers in involving their news staffs in digital journalism. By 2014, only three of the more than one thousand television stations broadcasting local news across the United States were charging for access to their websites, and the audiences for local stations' websites were not much larger than those for their television newscasts.

An annual survey by Hofstra University Professor Bob Papper for the Radio Television Digital News Association showed that, in 2013 and 2014, some local television stations were beginning to move faster to beef up their websites' content, to push their staff to promote them on social media, and to design strategies for their stations' news on digital media, especially mobile devices. Yet Papper found that only 22% of local television newsroom content was web-only, only a few station employees worked full time on their websites, and only 20% of the station's news directors had responsibility for their websites. Just as they do with televised newscasts, some local stations share websites to hold down costs.

KNXV-TV, the ABC affiliate in Phoenix, is one of the more aggressive local stations on the Internet. Its digital media staff has been growing, and its reporters write website print versions of their television stories, post updates, and promote their work on social media. The station's website features news from its own staff; the Washington bureau of its owner, Scripps; and other sources.

What's happened to news on radio?

With the notable exception of public radio and a relatively small number of all-news commercial radio stations scattered around the country, there is very little news on American radio stations today.

Most of the 11,343 commercial AM and FM radio stations in the United States in 2014 broadcast no news or only a short two-to-five-minute news bulletin from ABC Radio or CBS Radio at the top of each hour of their music, sports, or talk programming. The several hundred stations that label themselves as "news/talk/information," according to the Pew Research Center, are ``filled with more talk than news, much of it nationally syndicated" conservative personalities such as Rush Limbaugh, Sean Hannity, Michael Savage, and Glen Beck.

Only in nineteen cities are "all-news" commercial radio stations broadcasting news throughout the daylight hours or around the clock, mostly sandwiched between frequent traffic, weather and sports reports, and commercials. On some of those stations and their websites, much of the news is repurposed from broadcast networks, news services, and local newspapers, although each of the stations also has a few reporters on the street.

By contrast, the most ambitious all-news stations—nearly all of them owned and operated by CBS Radio in large cities—including New York, Boston, Philadelphia, Detroit, Chicago, San Francisco, and Los Angeles—have relatively large reporting staffs and sometimes cover more local news than commercial television stations in the same cities. On their websites, the CBS all-news stations combine their own news stories and multimedia with audio and video from CBS News.

The largest amount of national news on the radio is broadcast by nonprofit National Public Radio (NPR) through its estimated 900-member public radio stations across the country. In addition to news bulletins on the hour, NPR broadcasts two-hour-long morning and evening news programs every day, with local news produced by the local member stations inserted into each hour. The audiences for *Morning Edition* on weekday mornings (nearly seven million listeners each day) and *All Things Considered* in the afternoons (more than five million) are the largest for radio news, competitive with the audience for each broadcast television network news program and much bigger than the total cable television news audience. NPR newscasts include news stories from NPR's own staff of several hundred located in its Washington, DC newsroom, seventeen bureaus in the United States, and seventeen other bureaus around the world—and from NPR member stations. Only a relative handful of news organizations, such as the Associated Press, New York Times, Wall Street Journal, Bloomberg, and CNN, have more national and foreign news bureaus. Local news coverage varies widely among public radio stations, which mix news with public affairs, cultural, entertainment, and music programs. The majority of public radio stations have only a few, if any, local news reporters. Only the largest public radio stations and groups of stations—including WNYC in New York and New Jersey, Chicago Public Radio, Minnesota Public Radio, Southern California Public Radio, and Oregon Public Broadcasting in the Pacific Northwest—maintain sizeable newsrooms and cover their communities meaningfully on the radio. Some public radio stations are collaborating with each other and with start-up nonprofit digital news organizations to increase local news coverage.

Why doesn't public broadcasting play a bigger role in American news coverage?

Americans provide comparatively little support for public broadcasting—an estimated $4 per capita in government funds and private donations combined. The roughly $400 million that Congress appropriates for public broadcasting each year amounts to $1.30 per US citizen—compared to an estimated $22 per capita in government spending on public broadcasting in Canada, about $80 in Britain, and more than $100 in Denmark and Finland. The federal money in the United States goes to the quasi- independent Corporation for Public Broadcasting. The CPB then gives grants to nonprofit public television and radio stations, most of which are licensed to colleges, universities, and other nonprofit organizations. CPB grants account for only a fraction of the budgets of most of those public stations—and only a tiny fraction for the largest stations. Most of their financial support comes from philanthropic, corporate, and personal donations and, in the case of a few large stations, the sale of programs they produce and syndicate to other public broadcasting stations. Many donations are credited on the air in what increasingly sounds to listeners as abbreviated advertisements.

Only a small amount of the CPB money makes its way into news. Three-fourths of CPB grant funds goes to public television stations, which, as we have discussed, do very little news reporting. Instead, the television stations spend most of their money on broadcast facilities, overhead, entertainment programming, and fundraising. Only a quarter of the CPB money—about $100 million each year—goes to public radio stations, even though they greatly outnumber public television stations. And most public radio stations' fundraising supports only very small news operations.

In recent years, the CPB has spurred a movement to increase local journalism on public broadcasting stations, investing more than $20 million in various projects since 2009. For example, to encourage collaboration among stations that could increase the impact of their news staffs and resources, as of 2014 the CPB had made grants to nine "Local Journalism Centers" in which a number of public radio and television stations partner on regional news coverage of subjects including agriculture in the Midwest, education in the South, the changing economy in Pennsylvania, energy in the mountain and prairie states, the environment in the Northwest, and immigration and border issues in the Southwest. Some of them have had difficulty collaborating effectively across distances, and two of the partnerships have disbanded. But the remaining seven—comprising fifty-five public radio and television stations—have been continuing the experiment.

What is 'digitally native' news?

Most news on the Internet still originates with digitally transforming traditional news organizations: newspapers, news services, and television and radio networks and stations. Digital forms of news they produce appear on their own news sites and reappear in many other places throughout the Internet. Fifteen of the twenty most-visited American news sites in 2012, as measured by Nielsen, were those of television and cable networks and newspapers and newspaper groups—including ABC, CBS, NBC, Fox, CNN, *The New York Times, The Washington Post, Wall Street Journal,* and Gannett, Tribune, and Advance newspapers. Several also had relatively large followings on Facebook and Twitter, according to comScore data. They're being read and followed by young adult web users, too; 17.6 million of the nearly fifty million total unique visitors to *The Washington Post*'s digital news sites in May, 2015 were aged 18 to 24.

At the same time, an increasing amount of digital news is being offered by start-up "digital native" news organizations that are only available on the Internet. Some are for-profit general interest websites with large audiences and increasingly well-known brands. Many others are relatively small nonprofit news organizations focused on niches like investigative reporting or community journalism.

Some of the for-profit digital native websites with the largest audiences began as aggregators of news content picked up from the websites of established media. The digital native sites have never paid those news media for that content, although they have helped drive some traffic to the originating news sites. Ezra Klein of the digital native site Vox, which aggregates some of the content it reworks into its explanatory journalism, with attribution to its original source, has noted that this is not a new practice. "*Time Magazine*, for instance, began its life as an aggregation shop," Klein wrote on the Vox site in 2015. "It promised, on behalf of the busy American, to climb through 'every magazine and newspaper of note in the world" for the news that its journalists rewrote each week in what became *Time*'s unique voice. ("How Vox aggregates" posted on Vox technology, updated by Ezra Klein April 13, 2015).

The Huffington Post, now owned by Internet pioneer AOL, has built one of the Internet's largest audiences by combining links to and rewrites of content from major news organizations with its own journalism, plus numerous blogs from unpaid contributors, about everything from politics and world news to parenting and health, plus a potpourri of popular recycled digital stories and videos about celebrities, entertainment, lifestyles, sex, animals, and what it labels "weird" occurrences. Among examples of its own original journalism, The Huffington Post's military affairs correspondent, David Wood, won a 2012 Pulitzer Prize for a series of feature stories on the lives of severely wounded veterans and their families. Arianna Huffington, the website's founder and CEO, has attributed its huge audience (200 million unique visitors a month in 2015, according to comScore) to a mix of hard and soft news, original and borrowed, which, she said in a 2014 digaday.com interview, makes it "a leader in terms of all the content people want."

The digital formula of The Daily Beast, founded and formerly published by celebrity journalist Tina Brown, has been very similar to that of The Huffington Post, which, along with Huffington herself, had once been seen as arch rivals of The Daily Beast and Brown. Now owned by IBT Media, the Daily Beast has featured a similar mix of links to content aggregated from other news organizations, contributed blogs, and entertainment features from around the Internet.

One of the newer aggregators, Mashable, has combined general and entertainment news content from other media with its own reporting on social media, technology, and business. One of the oldest, Yahoo News, part of the giant Yahoo! Web portal and search engine, has recently been expanding its original news and sports reporting, while hiring prominent journalists from newspapers and television. Its merged website with ABC News has featured mostly news from ABC and other news media.

Some for-profit websites started by tech entrepreneurs have built large audiences by analyzing web traffic data to determine what content would attract the most people. They often feature the same stories, photos, or videos that had gone viral on the Internet, with their own catchy headlines and garish display to attract the most traffic. BuzzFeed, for example, features trivia lists, animal features, and popular web videos, to which it has more recently added much more original journalism, including investigative reporting. Gawker Media mixes sensational news stories with celebrity gossip, animal features, and unusual occurrences. Hollywood-based TMZ specializes in gossip and titillating videos about entertainment personalities and other celebrities. All three have occasionally broken stories of great impact with information, recordings, or videos obtained from undisclosed sources. For example, TMZ posted both a video of then Baltimore Ravens football player Ray Rice punching his wife inside an elevator and an audio recording of then Los Angeles Clippers basketball team owner Donald Sterling making racist remarks.

In a way, these popular digital sites have followed in the footsteps of newspapers that long mixed original journalism with news stories from wire services, entertainment and lifestyle news, gossip columns, advice to the lovelorn, bridge and chess columns, comic strips, and astrology charts. The major differences were that newspapers have paid for all that content and their ratio of news to entertainment has been much higher.

Some newer digital native sites—such as Vox and FiveThirtyEight—specialize in explaining the news and analyzing noteworthy data in digitally innovative ways, in addition to aggregating other content. Some other start-ups like Syria Deeply have focused on a single subject with aggregated content from other media and their own blog posts. Those sites are all similar to explanatory, data analysis, and single-subject blogs on the digital sites of traditional news organizations, including *The Washington Post* and *The New York Times*, where Ezra Klein of Vox and Nate Silver of FiveThirtyEight, respectively, had previously worked.

There are also for-profit startup websites that primarily do original news reporting. Politico specialized in news about politics, government, and the news media for an insider audience, part of which has paid substantial subscription prices for its Politico Pro specialized information products. Business Insider focuses on business and technology, while Re/Code, bought by Vox in 2015, and Tech Crunch also cover technology. Salon and Slate, comparatively older digital magazines, feature staff-produced stories and blogs about politics, public affairs, culture, media, and entertainment. Vice, a Canadian print magazine that morphed into a digital upstart, covers some of the same subjects plus international stories, aimed at a younger audience, and has specialized in edgy videos, such as a series shot in 2014 in the company of extremist Islamic State in Iraq and Syria troops in the Middle East.

Fewer commercial digital-only news sites have specialized in local news, and only a few of them have survived. An exception is Hearst's SeattlePI.com, which replaced the *Seattle Post-Intelligencer* newspaper when it closed down in 2009. One of the newest independent for-profit startups, Billy Penn in Philadelphia, combines links to news produced by other Philadelphia media with its own reporting, entertainment features, and community events aimed at the city's growing population of young adults.

More numerous "hyper-local" for-profit news sites, resembling blogs with advertising, have been started by entrepreneurs in smaller communities and neighborhoods scattered around the country. Some, like the Local News Now sites in several Washington, DC neighborhoods, operate independently. Others collaborate with local newspapers; several dozen neighborhood sites in the Seattle area, for example, share story links and advertising sales with the *Seattle Times*.

Perhaps most significantly, startup digital native for-profit news sites have so far augmented rather than replaced increasingly digital traditional commercial news media. In fact, without them, much of the news content of the digital startups would disappear. In addition, the economic models that the newcomers are trying to establish—varying mixtures of venture capital, advertising, digital subscriptions, ticketed events, and digital services for commercial customers—have yet to prove more viable for the future than the changing economic models of older news media.

What are blogs and what happened to them?

Blogs, originally called weblogs, began in the 1990s as diary-like entries of information and opinion posted in reverse chronological order, with the most recent post first, on personal digital sites that could be accessed by anyone on the Internet—in other words, logs on the web. Blog readers could post comments and engage in dialogue with the blogger. The tens of millions of infinitely varied blogs on the Internet today also include photographs, videos, graphics, and links to other content on the Internet, with designed web pages and mobile device applications.

Journalists initially denigrated blogs as amateur musings by people in pajamas sitting at their home computers. But, over time, a growing number of independent bloggers, some working in newsroom-like groups, produced news and commentary that amounted to journalism about subjects on which they were or became expert, including economics, the law, technology, education, health, food, fashion, travel, parenting, and even the news media. Some of these blogs grew into widely followed sources of specialized news and comment, like SCOTUSblog about the law and the US Supreme Court, or Talking Points Memo about politics and public affairs, with their own staffs of journalists.

Some specialized bloggers eventually went to work for newspapers and broadcast media that merged the blogs into their news sites and expanded them with additional staff. At the same time, newspapers and broadcast media added more and more blogs by their own journalists, who post items throughout each day on incremental developments and inside information on such news beats as politics, international affairs, sports, business, technology, education, entertainment, and the media. News organizations also often use bulletin-like, staff-produced blog posts for minute-by-minute real time coverage of major breaking news events—from sensational crimes, terrorist acts, and natural disasters to political debates and election nights—until fuller stories can be pieced together.

A few blogs succeeded in their founders' ambitions of becoming major national digital native sites, including The Huffington Post and Gawker. Some smaller ones became hyperlocal news sites covering towns or neighborhoods for their fellow residents. Millions of others remain solo voices who may or may not mix newsy information with their commentary for relatively small audiences.

What do social media have to do with journalism?

Although none of the most popular digital social media communities are much more than a decade old, they are the fastest-growing ways to share conversations, messages, information, images—and, yes, news—on the Internet. We're talking about everything from the digital social networks Facebook (founded in 2004) and Twitter (2006) to photo-sharing Instagram (launched in 2010, bought by Facebook in 2012); video-sharing YouTube (started in 2005, bought by the web search engine Google in 2006); and cross-platform smartphone messaging WhatsApp (launched in 2009, bought by Facebook in 2014).

Millions of people using social media each day discover news that is being shared by other people and by news organizations, whether they are purposefully looking for it or not. Half of those using social media surveyed by the Pew Research Center in 2014 said they had shared news stories, photos, or videos at one time or another.

An example of the role and reach of social media explored by *The New York Times* in 2011 was the killing of terrorist leader Osama bin Laden in a US Special Forces raid in Pakistan. Rumors about it were widely shared on social media twenty minutes before confirmed reports were broadcast late at night on broadcast and cable networks—and an hour before President Obama announced it from the Oval Office. News of Obama's statement and photos people took of him speaking on their television and computer screens also filled social media.

A significant number of people also have used social media to share breaking news they are witnessing in person. In the Pew Research Center survey, 14% of social media users said they had posted their own photos of news events, while 12% said they had posted videos. Many residents of Ferguson, Missouri, for example, posted eyewitness information, photos, and videos on social media about the 2014 police shooting of black teenager Michael Brown and the protests and clashes with police afterward, helping to make it a heavily covered national story.

At the same time, journalists and their news organizations use social media regularly to monitor news developments, seek out news sources, and solicit and find information from their audiences. Perhaps most importantly, they also use social media to help distribute their journalism and attract larger digital audiences for it, as well as to measure and analyze those audiences. Many news organizations, for example, put catchy new headlines on digital versions of their stories to increase their chances of being shared on social media.

At the same time, social media have further fragmented digital traffic to news websites in what Cory Haik, then senior editor for digital news at *The Washington Post*, has called "the great unbundling of journalism." Digital news consumers, especially younger adults, have been increasingly clicking from social media links onto individual pieces of news organizations' journalism rather than looking at their home pages or the rest of their websites, where they may have stayed longer and consumed more content. By late 2014, Haik said, only one-third of the many millions of digital readers of *Washington Post* news content came directly to the home page of its news site, while one-third found individual stories through search engines like Google and Bing, and another third arrived via links on social media. And nearly all of the traffic to the newspaper's content on mobile devices, she said, came from social media and search engines.

In a relatively short time, social media have challenged search engines as the primary way news media try to reach digital audiences. Shaping stories and headlines to rank higher on search engine results—"search engine optimization"—was the first way newsrooms sought to increase digital readership. Now, finding ways to increase social media sharing of a news organization's content—"shareworthiness"—is just as important, if not more so. The dilemma for news media is weighing widespread social media sharing—"going viral"—against continuing to do journalism about serious subjects that may not be so popular.

Social media—like some blogs and news sites—also transmit misinformation, erroneous news stories, unfounded rumors, and purposeful disinformation. Some of the shared messages, photos, and videos from the chaotic 2014 street clashes in Ferguson, Missouri, for example, were unintentionally misleading about the actions of protesters and police or were misinterpreted as they were passed along on social media. In 2011, social media spread erroneous news reports that then congresswoman Gabby Giffords had died in the Tucson shopping mall shooting in which she was seriously injured. In 2013, the message-sharing site Reddit prominently posted unfounded rumors about who was responsible for the Boston Marathon terrorist bombings. The startup site Storyful (acquired in 2013 by Rupert Murdoch's News Corp.), which helps client news organizations authenticate news reports and videos that appear on social media, has found many of them to be hoaxes.

Who decides what is news today?

The process of determining what is news has always involved a variety of actors—from publicists, government officials, and others seeking to get information into the news media to journalists evaluating the newsworthiness of that information. What has changed is that the process has become much more complicated and involves many more people and new technologies. Editors and broadcast news producers who not long ago were the primary "gatekeepers" of what the public saw and heard as news have been replaced in part by the traffic directors and consumers of digital media.

The traffic directors include the leaders of digital native websites; the programmers of algorithms that determine what news is most easily found on search engines and shared on social media; the digital data analysts in news organizations who discover which content attracts the most traffic to their sites and how it arrives there; curators of personalized content digital media; and so-called "power user" digital news consumers who are most active in sharing what they like online. They all help decide what people first see when they click on websites or what pops up on the screens of their computers and mobile devices.

News consumers, for their part, have their own say in ways that include the Twitter feeds they follow, the Facebook pages and links they prefer, and the digital news alert subjects they select. Websites and social media increasingly try to feed back to consumers the kinds of content they have most often clicked on in the past, just as advertisers try to feed to them ads that fit the profiles their keystrokes have drawn over time.

Traditional news media gatekeepers still play a role by deciding what news their organizations cover, which is still the largest amount of news available to be shared digitally. But they lose much of their influence after that—as their content bounces around the Internet like a beach ball in a sports crowd.

So is everyone a journalist now? What is audience engagement?

Anyone with access to the Internet can share news and create journalism today, just as citizen contributors to the news media did in the pre-digital past with story tips and letters to the editor, but now much more directly in much greater volume. That does not necessarily mean that these people are or will become journalists, but they can play a significant role in shaping the content of journalism.

Most news organizations regularly monitor social media for news, photos, and videos shared by citizens, and they evaluate tips and images sent directly to them. Increasing numbers of news organizations also actively solicit information from their audiences through social media, as well as print, broadcast, and website appeals. Some reach out to selected groups of people to help them research specific subjects. Others, like *The Washington Post*'s PostEverything blog, accept, edit, and publish journalism from outside writers and citizens. All of this amounts to what is now called "audience engagement" with the news.

ProPublica, the New York-based national investigative reporting nonprofit digital news organization, uses social media to create communities of citizens to participate in its investigations. For its ongoing multiyear series of investigative stories about the quality of American health care, for example, ProPublica created a Facebook group of more than 2,000 people willing to discuss patient safety with each other and ProPublica reporters. It solicited 560 responses from people about harm done to them as patients and another 150 responses from health care providers willing to share their experiences and views about patient safety. ProPublica journalists checked out the information as part of their reporting of stories for the nonprofit's website and for news media partners that published and broadcast its stories.

Other news organizations—from newspapers like *The Washington Post, Miami Herald,* and *Charlotte Observer* to numerous public broadcasting stations—have tapped the Public Insight Network (PIN) database of volunteer audience members created by Minnesota-based American Public Radio. Journalists post queries to PIN participants to discover stories and to solicit information, interviews, and feedback for stories they already are working on. A number of public broadcasting stations used PIN queries of their audiences to select key issues and questions for candidates in their coverage of local elections in 2014.

In another audience engagement experiment, a number of public radio stations led by WBEZ in Chicago have asked audience members to pose questions about news topics; vote on suggested stories they want to explore; and then help journalists report them for a weekly radio program called "Curious City," which is being expanded by its founders into "Curious Nation." Public radio station WNYC has used a foundation grant for surveys and focus groups to identify concerns of New York City residents that might influence the station's news coverage. With a $3.9 million grant from the Knight Foundation, *The Washington Post, The New York Times,* and the nonprofit technology developer Mozilla have been exploring development of a Knight-Mozilla OpenNews monitored "publishing platform for readers" to share comments, information, articles, images, and other audience-generated content. *The Dallas Morning News*, which has been experimenting with reader-contributed blog posts about local news and lifestyle subjects, won a $250,000 grant from the Knight Foundation in 2014 to enable more citizens, particularly Hispanics, to use social media tools to help inform, shape, and act on Morning News journalism about education and other community concerns.

Other kinds of audience engagement appear to be designed as much to save money as to expand journalism. Some large audience websites—including The Huffington Post, Forbes, Medium, and Reddit—have solicited and published unpaid stories and blog posts from their readers to add to their content without increasing their costs. Over 90% of Medium's content in 2014, for example, consisted of unpaid contributions, according to digiday.com, a site that covers media and marketing. Huffington Post has faced complaints from freelance journalists about lack of compensation, and other sites have been embarrassed by errors, conflicts of interest, and racist and sexist posts by unpaid contributors, whose content is lightly edited, if at all.

In these and other still unpredictable ways, the relationship between the media and what journalism professor and media blogger Jay Rosen has called "the people formerly known as the audience" is evolving rapidly.

Will nonprofit journalism save the day?

Before digital technology disrupted their economic models, many commercial news organizations devoted significant resources to "public service journalism"—including extensive coverage of public affairs and investigative reporting—while still realizing extraordinarily large profits. However, as their advertising revenue fell sharply their news staffs and resources were cut deeply after the turn of the century, significantly reducing resources for coverage of local and state governments and issues, as well as investigative reporting.

To try to fill some of the resulting gaps, a number of journalists, backed by charitable donors, started small nonprofit digital news organizations focused on community, state, or national public affairs coverage and investigative reporting. In 2014, the Pew Research Journalism Project counted two hundred such nonprofit digital news organizations receiving about $150 million annually from foundations, universities, philanthropists, and other donors.

Many large donors said they acted to ensure the future of public interest journalism by funding nonprofit sites. San Diego businessman Buzz Wooley initially financed the Voice of San Diego for local news and investigative reporting. Texas venture capitalist John Thornton helped start the Austin-based Texas Tribune for state news coverage. And California philanthropists Herb and Marion Sandler underwrote ProPublica for national investigative reporting. Other donors have backed nonprofit news sites covering specialized subjects, including the environment (Inside Climate News), criminal justice (The Marshall Project), health (Kaiser Health News), and education (Chalk Beat). Still others have supported ideologically oriented nonprofit sites, such as Media Matters, which reports on the news media from a liberal point of view, and Watchdog.org of the Franklin Center for Government and Political Integrity, for which a network of independent journalists in state capitals across the country report from a conservative point of view.

National and local philanthropic foundations—led by the John S. and James L. Knight Foundation, endowed with the Knight family's newspaper chain inheritance, and the Ethics and Excellence in Journalism Foundation, funded by Oklahoma's Gaylord newspaper publishing family—have helped finance many of the nonprofit digital news organizations. In just two of many examples, Knight and several California-based foundations have backed the state and national journalism of the Berkeley-based Center for Investigative Reporting, while Knight and the Pittsburgh Foundation helped start Public Source for investigative reporting in Pittsburgh and Pennsylvania.

Much of the journalism produced by nonprofits has been published and broadcast by commercial news media who collaborate with them. Investigative reporting by ProPublica and The Marshall Project, for example, has appeared in newspapers including *The New York Times, The Washington Post,* and *Los Angeles Times,* and on commercial and public television networks and public radio. Journalism produced by Pennsylvania's Public Source and The Texas Tribune, among a number of regional nonprofits, has been published and broadcast by news media throughout their states. Most of them have given their journalism to commercial news media free of charge. This has provided the nonprofits with much larger audiences than they would otherwise have, and it has given budget-conscious commercial news media significant additional journalism at little or no cost.

Some nonprofits have been working even more closely with public radio and television stations, including the collaboration between the inewsource.org investigative reporting nonprofit and the public station KPBS in San Diego, which we mentioned earlier. For example, the I-News investigative reporting nonprofit in Colorado has merged with Rocky Mountain PBS to produce news on its stations throughout the state. The *St. Louis Beacon* has merged its nonprofit newsroom with that of St. Louis Public Radio. And the Seattle-based Investigate West nonprofit collaborates on radio and television reports with public stations in the state of Washington. All of them are primarily supported by donors to public broadcasting.

Journalism produced by nonprofit news organizations has had a notable impact across communities and states in recent years, prompting reforms and drawing attention to such issues as local school performance, environmental problems, government malfunctions and corruption, and sexual assaults on college campuses. A number of nonprofits have won major regional and national journalism awards, including Pulitzer Prizes, usually dominated by commercial news media. ProPublica won 2010 and 2011 Pulitzers for national and investigative reporting, respectively, and Inside Climate News, which did not even have a physical newsroom at the time, won a national reporting Pulitzer in 2013 for its investigation of an environmentally damaging oil spill in Michigan.

But most news nonprofits remain financially fragile. Their leaders must constantly search for new kinds of financial support beyond the foundations and big donors who gave them their starts. The Institute for Nonprofit News, founded in 2009, helps more than one hundred national, regional, and local nonprofit news site members create collaborations, trains them in business practices and fundraising, and offers low-cost back-office services. Many local and statewide nonprofit news sites are trying to build broad-based local fundraising and memberships, similar to public broadcasting stations. *The New Haven Independent* website, for example, now raises 70% of its support locally. The Knight Foundation gave a $1.2 million grant in 2014 to the Voice of San Diego and the MinnPost local news nonprofit in Minneapolis-St. Paul to help them grow their local membership models.

The Texas Tribune, founded in 2009, has become one of the largest-staffed and financially strongest nonprofit digital news sites. Its staff of forty produces state government, politics, issue and investigative reporting, and interactive databases of Texas government and demographic information. With initial investor John Thornton, Evan Smith, the Tribune's CEO and editor in chief, has tapped the state's considerable wealth for philanthropic donations, paid memberships, paid-attendance events with newsmakers, and abundant corporate sponsorships on its website and for its events. The Tribune took in $5.1 million in revenue in 2013, including $1.16 million in corporate sponsorships, $1.13 in event income, and nearly $700,000 in memberships.

But studies of local and state nonprofit startups show that a majority of them have continued to struggle with budgets well under $1 million a year and staffs of fewer than half a dozen people, although some have punched above their weight with the impact of the journalism they produced.

How are some universities producing journalism, rather than just teaching it?

At the same time, a growing amount of nonprofit public service journalism is now being produced by students in some university journalism schools. Their stories and multimedia are being published and broadcast by newspapers, television, and radio stations and news websites in many cities and states where they are located, helping to fill some of the gaps in news media coverage of local communities, state governments, business, the environment and other subjects, in addition to investigative reporting. These students have been doing professional-level journalism while learning how to do it.

Students at the University of Maryland's Merrill College of Journalism, for example, have covered state and federal government news for Maryland newspapers from college-run bureaus in the state capital of Annapolis and Washington, DC. Other universities with statehouse bureaus in which students have produced stories for news media in their states include Boston, Illinois, Kansas, Missouri, and Montana. Student reporters, including those working part-time or on internships for news organizations, accounted for one of every six reporters working in statehouse news bureaus in 2014, according to a Pew Research Center study.

Students at Arizona State University's Walter Cronkite School of Journalism cover state and federal governments and issues, business, and sports news for Arizona news media from bureaus in Phoenix, Los Angeles, and Washington, DC. They produce a nightly half-hour regional newscast for Arizona's largest public television station, which became part of the

Cronkite School in 2014. In January 2015, Cronkite students produced a half-hour documentary on heroin abuse in Arizona that was simulcast on every television and radio station in the state. The Cronkite School also is the base for the annual foundation-supported News21 national student investigative reporting project, in which about thirty selected students from twenty universities produce multimedia stories about such subjects as food and transportation safety, voting rights, gun laws, and veterans affairs that have been published and broadcast by news media throughout the country. Students at Northwestern University's Medill School of Journalism work in a Medill news bureau in Chicago and a national security reporting project in Washington, DC. Recently graduated masters journalism students at Columbia University have covered local government, education, energy and environment for its news websites. Annenberg School students at the University of Southern California run the Los Angeles digital news site Neon Tommy. Students at the City University of New York and New York University staff neighborhood news blogs in New York City boroughs. In Ohio, students at Youngstown State University, the University of Akron, Kent State University, the University of Cincinnati, and Cuyahoga Community College intern at Youngstown State's TheNewsOutlet.com, which contributes community news to local news media. And Florida International journalism students staff the South Florida News Service, working with editors at the *Miami Herald, Sun-Sentinel,* and *Palm Beach Post*, which publish their stories.

All of this is part of a movement by some journalism schools toward what advocates call a "teaching hospital model" for professional journalism education, similar to university law school clinics and university teaching hospitals in which law and medical students gain real-life experience. Although academic leaders in some universities have ignored or resisted the trend, philanthropic foundations have focused their journalism education funding on schools experimenting with the teaching hospital model. Not surprisingly, both commercial and nonprofit news media have welcomed the professional quality journalism these programs have provided them at no cost. And the journalism students have been better prepared to step into multimedia news positions in rapidly changing newsrooms.

What is this about collaboration among news media? Haven't they always been competing with each other?

Until late in the twentieth century, it was almost unthinkable for one news organization to share its journalism with another one. Local newspapers in multinewspaper cities and states competed fiercely with each other, as did television stations and networks. There is still competition today to be first with news and to be known for exclusive stories, but there is also an extraordinary amount of collaboration—and not just by nonprofit news sites and university journalism schools with commercial news media. It has become an economic necessity for commercial news media.

Eight of Ohio's largest newspapers, for example, have regularly shared each other's stories, reducing costly duplication of coverage of statewide news. Five Texas newspapers—in Austin, Dallas, Fort Worth, Houston, and San Antonio—also have shared some stories, giving each paper journalism it wouldn't have otherwise. *The Baltimore Sun* and *The Washington Post* have traded coverage of their cities' sports teams. *The Post* and the Texas Tribune have a news-sharing agreement. Gannett's ninety newspapers and *USA Today* have shared news content and collaborated on national reporting projects. The digital news sites of Scripps' nineteen television stations do the same thing.

Local newspapers and television and radio stations in a number of cities have collaborated with each other on news, traffic, and weather reports. In New Orleans, television station WVUE has provided weather reports and news videos to the *Times-Picayune* and its website, and the newspaper has collaborated with the station on news and investigative reporting. NBC-owned television stations in Chicago, Miami, Los Angeles, New York, Philadelphia, and San Diego have collaborated with local nonprofit news organizations on everything from breaking news to investigative projects, providing the nonprofits with financial assistance and the stations with enterprise journalism they would not have produced on their own.

Nonprofit news organizations including ProPublica, The Texas Tribune, and Washington, DC-based Center for Public Integrity have encouraged other news organizations of all kinds to take stories and data from their websites to produce localized versions for their own audiences. ProPublica has even posted a "reporting recipe" step-by-step guide for some of its stories for the benefit of other news media.

Collaborations also have provided newspapers and broadcasting media with in-depth news about specialized subjects that they may no longer be able to cover extensively themselves. The Kaiser Family Foundation's non-profit Kaiser Health News has produced health care news published and broadcast by newspapers and public radio stations throughout the country. Two of the first three investigations of criminal justice issues produced by The Marshall Project nonprofit on its 2014 launch were published by *The Washington Post*. ProPublica's Pulitzer Prize-winning investigation of deaths at Memorial Medical Center in New Orleans in the aftermath of Hurricane Katrina was first published in *The New York Times Magazine.*

Whatever became of objectivity in journalism? Is credibility a better goal?

"Objectivity" is an often misunderstood journalism value. For too long, it was often thought to mean "just the facts" or "balanced" news reporting, avoiding any informed judgments by journalists. In that sense, Edward R. Morrow of CBS was not being objective in attacking McCarthyism. *The Washington Post* was not being objective in determinedly investigating how the Watergate burglary involved high-level political crimes that brought down a President. *The Guardian, The Post,* and *The New York Times* were not being objective in judging for themselves which of the NASA surveillance secrets revealed by Edward Snowden would be published by them. News organizations are not being objective in deciding to give much more weight to the scientific evidence of manmade global warning than to the nay-saying of some interest groups and politicians. Nor are they being objective in regularly fact-checking what politicians and officials say and then rating their truthfulness.

In the digital age, it is clearer than ever that there are sometimes only one or often many more than two sides to most stories, that false balance does not equate truth, and that context, explanation, informed judgment, and even point of view and "voice" can all be part of credible journalism. Credibility is what matters most for individuals and news organizations pursuing truth through journalism. Accuracy, fairness, open-mindedness, independence of power and ideology, and transparency about sources and methods whenever possible are among the news values that allow the audience to judge the credibility of journalism. In *The New Ethics of Journalism: Principles for the 21st Century,* Tom Rosenstiel and Kelly McBride say this means to "show how the reporting was done and why people should believe it." And they add that, when necessary, anyone committing journalism should make clear "whether you strive for independence or approach information from a political or philosophical point of view."

What is accountability journalism and its role in news media today?

Investigative reporting that gives voice to the voiceless in our society and holds accountable those with power over the rest of us has played a growing role in American journalism since

Watergate. A number of newspapers and television networks, even after drastic downsizing in recent years, still have assigned journalists to do investigative reporting as a specialty or on their beats. Increasing numbers of television stations have expanded their investigative reporting, even though much of it may be "watchdog" consumer investigations for competitive branding. And, as we've discussed, a number of nonprofit startups have primarily done investigative reporting, which they have shared with other news media.

The Investigative Reporters and Editors organization, with about 5,000 members, has been training more reporters at more news organizations than ever before. Digital technology has given reporters unprecedented access to data and other sources of information and enabled computer-assisted analysis of what they have found. Collaboration among news media has enabled sharing of shrunken staff and resources and wider exposure for investigative reporting.

Accountability journalism encompasses traditional investigative reporting but much more. It includes fact-checking political speech, digging into digital data, and aggressive beat coverage to reveal as much as possible about what is really going on in every aspect of American society—from national security, government, politics, business, and finance to the environment, education, health, social welfare, culture, sports, and the media industry itself. Accountability journalism has exposed, among much else, local, state, and national government corruption; frauds committed by businesses and charities; citizen abuse and unwarranted shootings by police; unpunished child molestation by Catholic priests; performance-enhancing drug use and spousal abuse by professional athletes; neglect of military veterans' medical problems by the US Veterans Administration; and plagiarism and fabrication by journalists and authors.

Accountability journalism has prompted change and reform. In one example, a 2013 investigation by the *Milwaukee Journal-Sentinel* found that newborn screening supervised by hospitals and state agencies across the country was failing to have hundreds of thousands of blood samples examined by laboratories in time to save babies from life-threatening conditions that could have been corrected. Hospitals and states soon changed their procedures, crediting the newspaper.

The widespread criticism of the news media for not being more aggressive in digging into the Bush administration's rationale for going to war in Iraq or Wall Street's financial manipulations leading to the 2008 financial meltdown shows that Americans have had high expectations for accountability journalism. However, practicing it can be challenging, especially in places around the country where newspapers no longer have sufficient staff or resources, television stations have not increased their investigative reporting, and no one has started an investigative nonprofit.

Then what is advocacy journalism and what role does it play?

Advocacy journalism seeks to achieve certain outcomes. Editorial pages and opinion columns and many blogs are advocacy journalism. News organizations whose owners use them to promote their own ideological and political views—such as Fox News on politics and Univision on immigration reform—are engaged in advocacy journalism, as are the news websites of advocacy groups like Human Rights Watch and the Committee to Protect Journalists.

Advocacy journalism can still inform while it advocates. The best newspaper editorials and opinion columns, for example, are based on reliable, sometimes revelatory reporting. Some accountability journalism can be seen as advocating change while revealing societal problems and wrongdoing. Avowed advocacy groups also can produce credible journalism about special interest subjects. Human Rights Watch and the Committee to Protect Journalists, for example, each have sizeable staffs of researchers and writers producing professional reporting that is often relied upon by the rest of the news media.

But some news sites produced by other advocacy groups—such as the conservative Heritage Foundation's Daily Signal and the liberal Center for American Progress's Think Progress—are more propaganda than journalism. Some groups, like the conservative Franklin Center for Government and Public Integrity, do not disclose their ideology or funders as they seek news media publishing partners. Transparency of purpose and funding is essential for judging the credibility of advocacy journalism.

Why do journalists sometimes use anonymous sources? How dependent is journalism on "leaks"?

The most credible journalism is transparent about its sources, identifying them whenever possible. However, especially in investigative reporting, sources can be reluctant to be identified for fear of losing their jobs or even coming to harm. Journalists make agreements to treat them as confidential sources whom they promise never to identify without being released from their agreements.

Famously, much of the Watergate reporting by Bob Woodward and Carl Bernstein of *The Washington Post* depended on such confidentiality agreements with sources who reached all the way up in the government to senior officials in the Nixon White House. None of those sources were identified while they were still alive. The Watergate stories usually referred to them only as "informed sources." With the exception of former FBI official Mark Felt, referred to until near his death only as "Deep Throat," *Post* editors knew the identities of all the Watergate sources, as editors should in judging the credibility of sources and stories.

Today many news organizations also require that anonymous sources be described, without violating confidentiality agreements, in ways that help audiences judge their reliability. Hence news stories often refer to "a senior government official" or "a source with knowledge of the investigation."

Because that still presupposes considerable trust of journalists and news organizations, anonymous sources should not be overused, as they too often are, just to avoid the trouble of persuading a source to go on the record. Government officials are especially eager to not be identified, even in routine stories, as the sources of "leaks."

Journalism in our democracy depends on officials being forthcoming with information about the people's business, including leaks from anonymous sources—whether authorized by government itself to reveal sensitive information without taking political responsibility, or by individual government officials who strongly believe the information should be made public. This is especially true of information classified as secret, the dissemination of which is legally risky for government employees. The federal government has been much more aggressive in trying to stop unauthorized leaks of classified information since the September 11, 2001, terrorist attacks.

During the Obama administration alone, six government employees, plus two contractors including the fugitive NSA leaker Edward Snowden, were subjects of felony criminal prosecutions for leaking classified information to the press under a 1917 Espionage Act, compared to three such prosecutions in all previous US administrations. In one of those investigations, the government secretly seized two months of call records for twenty telephones lines and switchboards in Associated Press bureaus in New York, Washington, DC, and Hartford, Connecticut, used by more than one hundred AP journalists on bureau, home, and mobile phones.

Journalists, of course, have a responsibility to do additional reporting to determine the veracity and context of information from leaks. More often than people realize, what may appear to be a purposeful leak is actually the product of a journalist aggressively seeking and gathering information from numerous sources and piecing it together like a puzzle. That was how, for example, *The Washington Post*'s Dana Priest discovered the US Central Intelligence Agency's secret prisons for the interrogation of terrorist suspects in countries in Eastern Europe and Asia.

So is the relationship between journalism and government adversarial or cooperative?

An important role of American news media is to hold government accountable for its actions, while government at all levels tends to be secretive and politically sensitive. This can lead to conflict over access to information, from the news media's point of view, and over what the news media decide to report, from government's point of view.

Despite widespread freedom of information laws, US federal, state, and local governments have become steadily more sophisticated about using media relations operations, bureaucratic hurdles, and digital technology to control what information they release and what they withhold. They have made it increasingly difficult for the news media to reach officials without going through protective press officers, and they have learned how to use social media and government websites to reach the public directly with information they believe to be favorable. News media have countered by becoming more aggressive with Freedom of Information requests, including informing the public when they are being stonewalled, and by scraping the Internet for useful data from which government performance patterns can be discerned with computer-assisted reporting.

There are times when news organizations do cooperate with government to protect human life or national security by delaying or withholding publication or broadcast of certain information, such as aspects of ongoing law enforcement activities, military actions, or covert intelligence operations. However, because of the First Amendment and the US Supreme Court decision in the Pentagon Papers case setting a very high bar for prior restraint on publication, those decisions are made by the news media alone, even after consulting with government.

In the case of the CIA's overseas secret prisons for the extralegal interrogation of terrorism suspects, for example, the executive editor of *The Washington Post* (this book's co-author, Leonard Downie, Jr.) decided to publish the story over strong objections made by President George W. Bush, the director of the CIA, and other senior officials in meetings at CIA headquarters and the White House. That led to the closing of the secret prisons, with the terrorism suspects brought as unlawful combatants to the military prison at the US naval base at Guantanamo Bay in Cuba. However, Downie also decided, after the discussions with government officials, not to name the eastern European countries where the CIA prisons had been secretly located to avoid disruption of other ongoing counterterrorism cooperation.

And how are private interests trying to manage news now?

While news organizations have been shrinking, corporate journalism has been growing. The number of corporate public relations specialists increased from 166,000 in 2004 to 202,500 in 2013, five times the number of newspaper reporters that year, according to the Bureau of Labor Statistics. And they have been increasingly working in corporate newsrooms that produce, in addition to traditional advertising and press releases, their own news-like stories and videos that appear as "sponsored" or "brand" journalism" in newspapers and on news websites and social media.

These corporate journalists have sources inside their companies, to whom the news media are often denied access, and the resources to produce sophisticated print, visual, and digital storytelling with subtle brand references that can be difficult to differentiate from other journalism. For a couple of months in late 2014, the marketing department of Verizon Wireless experimented with a news-like website, called SugarString, full of Verizon-produced stories for consumers about mobile communications and digital technology, with only small "Presented by Verizon" labels at the bottom of the web pages.

Many newspapers and digital media—from *The New York Times* to Buzzfeed—have started their own money-making "content marketing" staffs, working separately from their newsrooms, to produce branded journalism for advertisers and other corporate clients that mimics news content. In this way, corporations are able to pay news media to produce what amounts to advertising but looks almost like news on their digital sites. The *New York Times* brand advertising staff, T Brand Studio, for example, has produced subtly branded print and digital journalism for Dell, Netflix, and United Airlines, among other clients.

How accountable are the news media and journalists? Does it matter how popular they are?

Journalists usually rank near the bottom of surveys of popular opinion about various professions—just above advertising salespeople, politicians, lobbyists, and car salespeople in Gallup's annual poll. This could be attributed, in part, to journalists reporting unpleasant news, as well as information that clashes with the views of many in their audience. In addition, the missteps of the news media—errors, bias, plagiarism, and fabrication—are now more exposed than those in most other professions, except perhaps politics.

More important than popularity, in our view, is the credibility of journalism, whether or not it makes audiences uncomfortable. Journalistic credibility is dependent on news media accountability, which has actually increased in the digital age. Reporters, bloggers, and anyone else monitoring the news media can use the Internet to fact-check accuracy and expose plagiarism and fabrication, and anything they find can be shared widely on social media. This continual fact-checking of the news media—not unlike the news media's own increasing fact-checking of politicians and government leaders—could contribute to the perennial unpopularity of the press in opinion surveys. But it could also lead to increased credibility for those news media primarily engaged in verifiable journalism.

Just as important is that the judgments of their audiences in the digital echo chamber could matter more now to journalists than when they had been primarily dependent on the approval of other journalists, as sociologist Herb Gans observed during the heyday of self-admiring, comparatively autonomous journalism in the second half of the twentieth century. If journalism is indeed a profession, albeit without licensing or strict rules, it could benefit from the disciplining feedback, if not popular approval, from its clients and, increasingly, collaborators—the American public.

3

THE FUTURE

When will newspapers disappear completely? How about other news media like television news and radio journalism?

"Times are tough for the newspaper industry," writes one well-known media analyst. "Advertising is in a slump some analysts are calling the worst in twenty years. Profits are down substantially at many papers. Vacancies are being left unfilled and budgets are being squeezed if not slashed. Almost everywhere the mood is black. Perhaps because the business has been so lucrative for so long, the painful decline in advertising caught many in the industry unprepared, prompting a wave of anxiety about the future."

That quote is by Alex Jones, then the *New York Times* media reporter, and it is dated January 6, 1991. Worries that the news business is in trouble are nothing new. What might be new is both the scale of the crisis and the increasingly confident *predictions* of mass media extinction. A decade and a half into the twenty-first century, regular forecasts that the printed newspaper will one day (maybe even one day soon) vanish completely appear regularly. In mid-2014, digital theorist Clay Shirky published an analysis, titled "Last Call" and starkly subtitled "The End of the Printed Newspaper." In it, Shirky sarcastically argued "maybe 25-year-olds will start demanding news from yesterday, delivered in an unshareable format once a day. Perhaps advertisers will decide 'Click to buy' is for wimps. Mobile phones: could be a fad." Just a few days earlier, David Carr of the *New York Times* noted that "Print Was

Down, Now Out," and saw the spinning off of print divisions of multimedia conglomerates into stand-alone companies as the beginning of the end of newspapers in their current form. Predicting the demise of newspapers has a long pedigree: in *The Last Newspaper,* University of North Carolina Chapel Hill Professor Philip Meyer forecast that the last newspaper would be printed in 2043. Even the actor Cedric the Entertainer, appearing on the game show *Who Wants to Be a Millionaire*, speculated the final newspaper would roll of the presses in 2039.

All that said it seems unlikely that the newspaper itself will entirely vanish. Even the printed newspaper seems destined to last for a long time in one form or another, and the same goes for a variety of other news media formats. There is a long history of old technologies and media forms being repurposed, even when their original social function has been overtaken by technological, economic, or political changes. For instance, it might have been entirely reasonable to expect that radio would disappear after the invention of television; who, after all, would want to listen to words without pictures once words and pictures together were available? This, of course, is not what happened. Instead, radio shifted from being a national medium to a primarily *local* medium, ceding the national news agenda for several decades to television (indeed, in 1970 radio actually moved back into the national news business with the founding of NPR). Likewise, the printed newspaper did not vanish with the emergence of radio, despite the "press-radio war" of the 1930s. Instead both the printed newspaper and the growing power of radio news accommodated each other in a variety of unforeseen ways.

It's possible the current shift to digital is more profound than these older changes. It's possible that printed news published on a more-or-less daily basis, along with television news updates and radio news, really will vanish. The idea of digital *convergence*—the fact that what we're seeing online is not really the emergence of a new medium but the bundling of a variety of formats onto a single technological device—is a powerful argument that many news formats will disappear. But still—communications history teaches us that we shouldn't assume media formats entirely vanish, but rather that they often find surprising ways to accommodate each other. This is likely to be as true for whatever we call "television" twenty years from now as for printed news. Rather than disappear, television and print journalism will probably adopt new social roles.

What will the "new social roles" of these old media outlets be?

Text journalism will increasingly provide context for breaking news events, while visual journalism will focus more on discrete occurrences. And "auditory news" will also focus heavily on a combination of context and storytelling.

Let's start by distinguishing what we have long called visual news (television) and news based on text (primarily housed in newspapers but also in magazines), and by noting that these distinctions have become increasingly hard to justify over the last decade-and-a-half. And we'll probably continue to see the blurring of the lines with regard to these different formats, as journalists are increasingly trained to be proficient (or at least better than adequate) in multiple forms of media production as Internet news sites incorporate video, audio, graphical, and narrative text into single stories. There is also an increasing trend at many journalism schools to eliminate different media "tracks" for incoming students.

As lines between different media formats blur, it remains important to keep in mind that different types of media really do different things. They do different things for the reader, who gains different types of knowledge and gratification from each of the stylistic genres, as well as for writers and producers, who understand the journalism they produce in each of these different media formats in slightly different ways.

We can expect the social role of visual and video media to remain that of bringing readers dramatic or explanatory information, with an emphasis on the dramatic end of the moving-image spectrum. However, an increasing percentage of this content will probably be submitted by ordinary people rather than professional journalists. Even today, most news organizations use some amateur footage on a daily basis, with some, like Al-Jazeera Arabic, using as many as eleven hours of it per day. In addition, the line between newspapers and weekly or even monthly magazines will continue to shrink, with the amount of "interpretive" or "contextual" journalism continuing to grow. The social context of print, in other words, will shift even further toward narrative and explanation. And this shift will be paralleled online as well, with the continued rise of digital explanatory journalism, quantitative reporting, and contextual information graphics.

In other words, we might want to spend less time asking "when will print vanish?" and more time asking "what will print journalism continue to do that it does better than anyone else? How about televisual, audio, and data-oriented journalism? And how will these different forms make citizens either more or less informed about the world around them?"

Is there a magic bullet that is going to solve all of journalism's future revenue problems? Can "paywalls" save the news?

So what are paywalls? One way to think about them is as subscription fences that keep readers from freely accessing online news content. In many ways, the logic behind them is straightforward: just as a newspaper doesn't show up on your doorstep everyday without your paying for it (though it might if the newspaper delivery worker has made a mistake!) you increasingly can't gain access to some online journalism without spending money on it. But paywalls won't save the news. They will grow in importance and increasingly become less controversial. But they aren't a magic bullet. Indeed, the fact we even have to answer this question (and that we're calling the barrier between accessing news and paying for it a "paywall" rather than an online subscription) shows just how complex the future of journalistic business models really is, and how much has changed in our discussion of them over the years.

Hundreds of newspapers and magazines are now charging their readers for some form of "metered access." In other words, readers are charged for the news they consume after an initial round of free articles (usually somewhere in the range of ten articles per month). Even a few years ago, the idea that newspapers would charge their readers for news content was seen as economic heresy, or public interest apostasy, or both. In a 2009 article called "Now Pay Up," *The Economist* cited only a few papers, the *Wall Street Journal* and the *Arkansas Democrat Gazette* among them, which required readers to pay for access to news online. As is so often the case, the *New York Times* was at the forefront of a broader change in revenue strategy in the United States; the paper's introduction of a metered model in the Spring of 2011 led to a veritable stampede of other news properties to introduce metered access over the next several years. (Interesingly, the situation was quite different in Europe, with the *Times* of London, *Le Figaro, Handelsblatt* and *Berliner Morgenpost*—all major European newspapers—all introducing paywalls before the *Times*.)

But, how successful will this strategy be in the long run?

The answer to that question is actually fairly simple: meters and walls will provide news organizations with some revenue, but not nearly enough to maintain business operations and staffing levels as they have existed for the past fifty years.

Given that, it appears that many companies now charging for news have moved on from the paywall debate. They have moved beyond, in other words, debates about whether or not to force readers to pay for news: they should, these companies argue. Their strategy now revolves around figuring out how requiring consumers to register for access to content can also help news organizations build up an informational portfolio about the habits, needs, and interests of these very specific and news-focused consumers. News organizations have come to terms with the fact that *some* of their readers will be willing to pay for their content, and that these are the readers who are most likely to fund their journalism in other ways—whether they purchase additional bonus journalistic products (like access to archives) or sign themselves up for supplementary updates containing the latest breaking news. In addition, as these organizations learn more about the people who are paying for their content, they can turn around and use the data they collect from these people to better tailor advertisements to them. This has quite obviously been the strategy of the *New York Times*, but even that strategy wasn't enough to stop the *Times* from laying off, yet again, a large number of newsroom workers in the fall of 2014.

You said that hundreds of newspapers and magazines have instituted metered models for access to news content. Is that pretty much all of journalism, then?

No, it is far from being all of journalism. Many online-only publications, new journalistic startups, and many print-digital hybrids still offer all their content online for free, and will continue to do so for many years to come. Almost no broadcast news found online operates from behind a paywall, at least not yet.

Why?

There are a few possibilities here. Once upon a time, it might have been likely that some of these companies had a cultural aversion to charging their consumers money for news. The famous (if misquoted) phrase "information wants to be free" was often used to justify not charging readers money to access journalism on the Internet by claiming it would be impossible, or morally wrong, or both. Now, though, it seems like this rationale has largely disappeared. It no longer seems crazy to people that they pay for journalism on the Internet. But if this is true, and if the "culture of free content" really has faded away, then why isn't every news company charging for news? Why are some sites (including some of the most popular, like Buzzfeed, Vox, Upworthy, and Gawker) trying to pay for their journalism without asking their readers to pay as well? In part, the answers to this are economic: despite the growth in "direct payment models" for news, some outlets have continued to try to find other ways to subsidize the journalism they produce.

So what are these other models? What other options for future revenue growth are there?

The next few years will witness the continued growth of four major business models for online journalism: the direct payment model, the native advertising model, the venture capital model, and the traditional advertising model.

The first model, the direct payment model, eliminates the intermediary organizations that have long stood between news consumers and news producers. In earlier eras of news, the relationship between audiences and producers of news was mediated in two ways: first, by the business departments of newspapers who negotiated with outside advertisers and whose dealings were walled off from the editorial side of the company, and second, by the advertisers themselves. Advertisers paid news companies in order to be able to reach readers. The amount readers themselves subsidized news organizations through the direct purchasing of their content through subscriptions and newsstand sales has varied over time, but at least since the start of the twentieth century it never represented the majority of the newspaper's income. This is the American story; European newspapers normally receive much more income from subscriptions and sales, much less from advertising. In years to come, US newspapers are likely to see a greater and greater emphasis on readers paying directly for media content, including news content. Early 2013 was something of a landmark in this regard, as it marked the first time ever that annual circulation revenues passed advertising revenues at the flagship *New York Times*. How will news organizations make their money in the future? One answer is that readers will start to pay for the news they want directly.

The second possible future business model continues to rely more heavily on advertisements, but advertisements of a radically different kind. Called "native advertising," these ads are designed internally by creative teams at news organizations and then folded into publications so they largely "blend in" with actual news content. Not surprisingly, these native ads have been very controversial. They fundamentally rely on a sort of reader deception in order to be successful and also challenge the church-state separation between the editorial and business sides of many news companies. However, native advertising has also been very successful. Vox Creative and Buzzfeed Creative now work with advertisers to help them directly market their content, with Buzzfeed native advertising making a reported $120 million in sales in 2014. But it's not only new entrants into the journalism space that are dong this—even venerable outlets like the *New York Times* and *Washington Post* are. Internal teams at these publications also act as externally focused technology teams as well, with some even going so far as to build and market content management systems that can be sold to other news organizations and publishers of various kinds. How will news organizations make money? They will make money by making better advertisements and by blurring the lines between news and advertisements in the first place.

A third model for news is perhaps the oldest, as well as the simplest: online advertising, with ads popping up or appearing on webpages, ads that are clearly marked out from the rest of the content. But isn't traditional online advertising dying? These advertisements, publishers seem to have concluded, were a losing business and would never provide news organizations with enough revenue to make a significant dent in their expenses. But two developments over the last few years have changed this calculus enough to at least prompt news companies to revisit traditional online ads: the shift to the so-called "mobile web," and direct partnerships between online platforms like Facebook and select news publishers like the *New York Times*. Both these developments are related.

Mobile traffic now accounts for a larger percentage of overall Internet traffic than does PC-based traffic. Much of this traffic from mobile, in turn, is devoted to mobile apps rather than the "mobile web"—users spend a whopping 86% of their time on apps, versus only 14% on the web. The hope among many in the news industry is that the advertising experience will be substantially different enough on cellphones that it will make display ads more lucrative again. A second important development in the evolving conversation about online advertising emerged only in early 2015, with the debut of Facebook's "Instant Articles." Under the instant article program, a few select news organizations began to host content *directly* on Facebook, rather than uploading them to their own homepages and linking to them *off* Facebook. These instant articles promised faster load times and improved visual display, particularly on Facebook's mobile app. Facebook has also promised publishers 70% of the revenue generated by adjacent display ads, and access to the metrics about each article. If Facebook really does service better advertisements for news stories than these companies themselves do, the value of display ads might go up even as journalism organizations sacrifice some control over their content.

But even after all the hoopla about Facebook Instant Articles in the early summer of 2015, it's unclear if these articles would amount to anything more than an afterthought for most news organizations. Following the excitement about Instant Articles when they debuted, there were **no** new articles posted again for several months. This gap between the buzz surrounding the initial product launch and day-to-day reporting practice points out how hard it is to foster change in the world of journalism.

There is a fourth and final possible future business model for news—but we might call it less of a long-term model than a temporary holding strategy. Over the last few years, the largest funding streams for many of the newest digital news/entertainment hybrids have come from venture capitalists and Silicon Valley. In 2014, Andreessen Horowitz invested $50 million in BuzzFeed and valued it as being worth $850 million dollars. Vox Media was valued at $350 million in 2014. And while these venture capitalists (vcs) may be impressed with plans to create and market content-management systems (CMSs) and build native ads, the fact is that these investments are usually made on the basis of *predicted future growth.* In other words, Buzzfeed may not be worth $850,000,000 today, but it will be worth that much money one day in the future. Is that right? History has shown that vc valuations do not always pan out, and one of the biggest future questions for the startup news business will be to see how many of these infusions of cash pay off for journalism in the long run. There is the distinct possibility that the current value of these new digital media startups constitutes a bubble and that many of them could collapse in much the same way that "Pets dot com" did in the early 2000s. If this happens, this fourth option will not have amounted to much of a "business model" at all.

How about public funding for news? Could that somehow solve the journalism revenue crisis?

No, at least not in the United States. In the US at least, public funding for journalism won't grow in the years to come; in fact, funding levels will probably decline. But the government can affect news production in ways that go beyond simple funding.

The United States spends comparatively little money on public broadcasting: $3 per US citizen, compared to $22 per person in Canada, $80 in Britain, and $100 and more in Nordic countries. Direct public funding for the news media has found little political support in the United States and is not likely to find more. It seems far more likely that government funding for public journalism will decline in the future, especially if critiques of government spending continue in the manner they have for the past several decades. But while an increase in funding for journalism broadcast outlets seems unlikely, the federal government still faces a number of regulatory decisions that will less directly affect the future economics of news production and media content. One example of this is the recent skirmish over "network neutrality" (more often called "net neutrality") in the United States.

The debate over net neutrality basically involved an argument over the question of whether or not Internet service providers (ISPs) could institute tiered pricing for the preferential treatment of certain types of Internet traffic. Could Netflix strike a deal with Comcast, in other words, for its movies to be shown at higher speeds (and thus in higher quality) than the content over YouTube? Historically this type of tiered pricing hasn't been the norm online, but the explosion of video traffic and the increasing merger between digital and broadcast content called that rigid neutrality of the network into question. In 2015, however, the Federal Communications Commission decided to reclassify broadband services as a Title II communications service, reinforcing tacit network neutrality principles. When broadband service gets classified under Title II, that means that it is treated as a core communications service, which gives the FCC a stronger legal authority to regulate it. Because of this reclassification, principles of nondiscrimination of online traffic remained in force.

Now, what does all this have to do with the future of journalism? Forty or even twenty years ago, journalism organizations (particularly broadcasters) might have *wanted* to see network neutrality rules get overturned! They did, after all, produce the majority of broadcast news content and were well funded enough to pay for special treatment by Internet service providers. Those days, however, are long past. Indeed, some of the most interesting startup news organizations of the last few years have been startup *broadcasting* companies (like Fusion, which is a partnership between Walt Disney and Univision and aimed at the Hispanic market; and Vice, which in addition to online content also specializes in edgy video news from places like North Korea and Islamic State-occupied territory in Syria and Iraq). Given the fragmentation of today's journalism market, and the relatively high importance of new news organizations in plotting a future for news, government decisions to reclassify broadband as Title II can actually help emerging news organizations navigate the new digital landscape. If a new online-only digital news entrant like Vice decides they want to invest money in gathering news from hotspots around the globe, they can do so knowing that the journalism they produce will be treated just the same—in terms of streaming and download speeds—as news produced by an already established competitor.

The US government faces many media regulatory decisions that go beyond debates over net neutrality, of course. But focusing on this topic helps us understand that government regulation can impact the future financial fortunes of journalism organizations in ways that go beyond the (relatively limited) direct funding levels provided to direct news production. There are many ways that news media organizations can be subject to public intervention, even if we know that government funding levels won't be increasing anytime soon. Indeed, the distinction between public, nonprofit, and commercial media is getting more tangled than ever.

Will nonprofit news outlets become key players in the journalism landscape in the future?

In the future, not-for-profit news companies will produce only a small percentage of the journalism in the United States. However, it is also likely that this kind of journalism will have an above average impact on audiences and the public.

On the one hand, there are a growing number of nonprofit news organizations in the United States. These emerging organizations are having an impact both on journalism business models (because they provide a viable model for other news organizations to follow) and the health of democracy in the United States (because of the journalism they are actually doing). And yet, for all the good they provide for both journalism and the public, the finances of most nonprofit news organizations are fragile. They depend on unpredictable grants from national and local foundations, private donations, audience memberships, and fundraising events.

Much of the future of nonprofit news depends on actions taken by the Internal Revenue Service. For several years during the height of the journalism financial crisis (when legacy news organizations were cutting staff and circulation at a pace which far outstripped the creation of news business models) there was a common complaint launched against the IRS that its rules and guidelines made unclear what kind of nonprofit news would be okay. The IRS had not been in the habit of designating news organizations not-for-profits, and the more politicized nature of many of these early journalism companies made for some uncertainty. For a year and a half, pressure mounted on the government to clarify the IRS rules so news organizations would know where they stood. Much of the uncertainty about the nonprofit status of news organizations has dissipated in the past few years as the IRS has clarified its criteria for evaluating news organizations, and as they in general have gotten more used to the idea. But it is important to keep in mind that, ultimately, news organizations are not totally in control of whether they get to claim tax exemptions.

Even with an increasingly smooth path to 501(c)3 status, though, it still seems likely that only a portion of news and journalism will be produced through a strictly not-for-profit business model. There are at least two reasons for this. First, the dominant media structures in the United States have been resolutely for-profit for most of the last two centuries. When institutions and organizations remain in one particular mold for a long time, the tendency is for them to remain in that mold even amid many other changes. Scholars call this "path dependency." For most news organizations, the "path" has been one oriented around commercial profit. It is likely this commercial path will start to break down to some degree, but inertia remains a powerful force.

Second, much of the news produced by nonprofit news organizations like ProPublica is niche-focused and assumes a fairly high degree of interest in politics and public issues. Involved, engaged readers are the core audience of many of these nonprofit news companies. And while it is likely that there are citizens whose needs for in-depth news reporting are currently being unmet, it also seems likely that this number is (relatively) small. In other words, nonprofit media organizations have tended to produce specialty journalism. We might even call it elite journalism! And there is only so much elite interest to go around.

How are distinctions among nonprofit, for-profit, and public media becoming harder to draw?

There's an important addendum to the story we've laid out so far about public and other nonprofit media. Journalism scholars often write about public media in the United States as if it is an alternative to the corporatized, advertising-driven (and increasingly Silicon Valley-oriented) commercial press. However, these lines are quickly blurring, especially but not only in public radio. The vastly underfunded but relatively popular American public media system is turning to advertising, and to a variety of Silicon Valley-inspired organizational innovations, in order to make up for the shortfall of shrinking government support from the CPB (Corporation for Public Broadcasting).

Many of these developments are new and likely to evolve in the years ahead, and so these are just a few examples of the shrinking line between public and commercial journalism in the United States. Most of them are drawn from the world of public radio, where the changes in journalism and news seem the most pronounced, though the move of the iconic children's television show "Sesame Street" from PBS to HBO is emblematic of the larger pressures faced by public media outlets regardless of content type and media format.

Following the success of the podcast *Serial* in the fall of 2014, there has been a veritable podcast "gold rush," with a number of innovative new shows taking advantage of the fact that the FCC did not impose sponsorship guidelines on podcasts like they did over radio airwaves. For traditional, terrestrial public radio, the FCC limits the types of sponsorship that programs can receive and the length of the underwriting segments that can appear on air (usually limited to fifteen seconds). All this is done in order to keep public radio "commercial free." However, there are currently no guidelines for podcasts, which means that there are greater opportunities to raise revenue without running afoul of regulations.

According to one website that monitors public radio, "NPR's revenue from podcast advertising had doubled from fiscal year 2013 to 2014. Downloads of NPR's podcasts grew 40% over that time.... And NPR's podcast ad income from the first five months of this fiscal year has outstripped its take in all of fiscal year 2014." The podcast explosion also helped advance the business prospects of Radiotopia, a collective of digital-first audio programming which pioneered new story-driven shows and allowed its members to share technical and audience-growth expertise. Launched a few months before *Serial* in February 2014, Radiotopia was funded with a $200,000 initial grant from the Knight Foundation, raised over $600,000 in a Kickstarter campaign, and received an additional $1 million grant a year later.

Finally, we should mention PRX, perhaps the most far-reaching experiment in hacking the public radio paradigm. Founded in 2003, PRX acts as a digital "exchange" through which NPR stations can trade audio content, including finished programs as well as streaming audio. The goal of PRX is to inject digital savvy into what its founders see as the staid world of NPR. The most important contribution of PRX lies not in its content (though much of that content is excellent) or even in the notion of a digital exchange; rather it is really shaking things up because of its economic model and its overall worldview. One of PRX's projects is Matter, a public-media "startup accelerator" in San Francisco that began as a collaboration between PRX, the Knight Foundation, and KQED. Startup accelerators take small chunks of startup equity in exchange for mentorship and early access to capital; after a few months, the participants in the accelerator "graduate." While common to the world of Silicon Valley, it's clear that at this point we have left the world of old-fashioned public radio, with its CPB funding reliance on congressional appropriations, pledge drives, and tote bags far behind.

Now it's possible that none of these initiatives will last very long. On the other hand, some of them may turn out to be very successful. What matters is not so much any individual initiative; rather it should be clear that even the relatively sedate world of public broadcasting is changing rapidly and will likely change more in the future.

What about public media organizations in other countries, like the British Broadcasting Corporation? What will their future be like?

The British Broadcasting Corporation (BBC) along with other public media organizations in other countries, is funded differently than the predominantly American news companies we have discussed so far. Even public media in the United States is quite different from the BBC. We already noted how little money the United States spends on publicly funded journalism in comparison to other nations. But even the wealthiest, most powerful public service broadcasters are vulnerable to larger changes in journalism. Take the BBC, for instance. 96% of Britons help subsidize the BBC through their annual service fee, a tax that every British household with television service is obliged to pay, which makes the network of stations and websites run by the BBC both uniquely important and uniquely subject to political pressures. Conservative politicians have long decried the service fee as an anathema and a regressive tax on the public. And the directors and CEOs of other media outlets in the UK have complained that the power of the BBC gives it an unfair advantage in the emerging marketplace of digital news—it's hard to compete with the BBC online, in other words.

The BBC charter is up for renewal in 2016, which means that politicians and media figures will be debating its future intently. Some of the items up for debate include: Should the BBC produce entertainment programming or focus more on its core mission? Should the license fee be eliminated or modified? How should the corporation be governed and regulated? The BBC is a major producer of news both in the United Kingdom and in the English-speaking world, and the debate over its future is likely to have a major impact on the future of journalism, even in the United States.

What about streaming video in general? Will that become an increasingly popular way to get news?

Almost certainly it will. In general, news videos are able to command premium advertising prices (usually in the form of a pre-roll clip at the start of story) in the way that textually oriented stories are not. As web traffic speeds increase, we can also expect the ability to stream high-quality video, including news video, to grow. The news experience online will become increasingly visual.

That said, it is likely that much of this footage will not resemble the traditional "local-network news set experience." Rather we will see the emergence of decidedly new visual formats, ones that include raw footage from citizen journalists on the scene of major events, infographics and other animated data-rich material, commentary, and the integration of social media into the televisual format.

So it seems like you've been avoiding a straight answer about this: What's the business model for this new/old journalism hybrid?

There probably won't just be one model. Subscriptions, metered walls, native advertisements, technology services, Silicon Valley investments, and government and foundation funding will probably all provide revenues to news organizations in the years to come. The biggest financial change for journalism organizations of the future will be their increasing need to diversify their funding streams. The days of a single primary source of revenues to support newsgathering are over.

What does the "rise of mobile" mean for the future of journalism?

By "rise of mobile," news industry executives and journalism analysts refer to the very real fact that more than half of all Internet use now is through mobile devices, and that for a growing number of news publishers more half their traffic comes from mobile devices. But while the devices through which journalism is consumed are changing, many news publishers have yet to settle on an appropriate strategy for dealing with these changes. Not a lot of news is "optimized" for mobile devices, which means it is often hard to read and interact with on iPhones and Android devices. And think about how you find content on your mobile device. More likely than not you find it through an app that is wired into a social network (Facebook, Twitter, etc.) rather than searching for it on Google.

The business of mobile news is also changing. As we might gather from the thoughts above, the relationship between journalism and social media changes in a mobile-first universe, with publishers more dependent on staying in their good graces. And the way publishers get money in a mobile marketplace also changes. Data shows that customers are slightly more willing to pay for news on mobile devices but the market for display advertising is even worse than on desktops; screen sizes are tiny and ads are almost certainly seen as more of an annoyance than anything.

And so expect journalism to continue to wrestle with the implications of mobile technology in the years ahead. One interesting question will be whether journalists can not only adapt to mobile technology but whether their need to adapt to *this* technology will finally convince them that they need to be constantly anticipating the next digital disruption to come along, a disruption that will likely force them to grapple with the production and distribution of their news content in new ways.

Is there a big difference between local and national news coverage when it comes to the future of news?

It's hard to be totally certain about anything related to the future of news. But if there's one thing we can say with some degree of confidence, it is that national (and even international) news organizations and brands will probably be more economically successful than local or regional news outlets. It is more likely that the *New York Times* will be around in twenty years than many local newspapers. From the closure of the *Rocky Mountain News* in 2009; to the slashing of home delivery and even the number of days per week the newspaper is printed for distribution in cities like Detroit, New Orleans, and Cleveland; to the bankruptcy of large regional chains like Philadelphia Newspapers LLC, the Journal Register Company, the Tribune Company, and Sun Media Group, regional news organizations have been decimated in ways that their more global counterparts have not.

But why should this be? Hasn't the Internet made it easier to give consumers of information exactly what they want to watch or read in a targeted fashion? Why aren't local and regional news outlets looking at a bright future? One answer might be that local news websites aren't "sticky" enough. Local news websites account for only 15% of all news traffic on the web, with 85% going to national news sites; in terms of entire web traffic, local news counts for one-half of one percent. As one media scholar aptly put it, "local newspaper traffic is just a rounding error on the larger web." What's even worse is that local news websites still aren't doing a lot of the things their larger national rivals are doing—their web pages load slowly, they often look terrible and are awful to navigate, they are loaded with obnoxious advertisements, and they aren't personalized. These days, national news websites also test out different story headlines simultaneously in order to see which one will draw the most readers—what people in the industry call "A/B testing." Local news sites rarely do testing of this kind.

There are at least four other explanations for the relative dearth of local media success, beyond the very real fact that many of their websites are terrible. It is possible that national and international brands will simply continue to have a larger readership (or potential readership) and can thus command higher advertising rates on the open market. Related to this, it is also possible that the differences between advertising rates have more to with the demographic characteristics of *New York Times* and *Wall Street Journal* readers—distributed over a larger potential pool of readers, these companies can more easily target their content to the most valuable audiences. A third explanation might be that global and national news companies like the *Times* and *Washington Post* are family-owned and have thus been able to stand up to the vicissitudes of the turbulent journalism market.

The fourth and final explanation is the most seductively simple, but we need to be aware that even here there is contradictory and confusing information. Maybe people simply **care more** about national and international news. When the hyperlocal news organization Patch shut down most of its operations in late 2013, one of the reasons offered for its failure was that people simply didn't care about local news; they care far more about events in the Middle East than events at a local Middle Eastern restaurant. But the data is unclear. Perhaps Patch folded not because people don't care about local news, but because it was poorly designed and poorly run. Perhaps, in fact, people only care about international news when they understand how it relates to their local circumstances. Maybe people care about international news *more* when they see how it relates to their daily lives.

Even if that's the case, though, it doesn't help us answer our question: *Why* are local news websites having such a tough time? A final interesting data point lies in what we might call the "nationalization" of the American news business. Forty years ago, there were many strong regional newspapers, and a few upper tier regional papers that had national ambitions—the *New York Times*, the *Washington Post*, *USA Today*, the *Los Angeles Times*, and perhaps the *Chicago Tribune* or the *Philadelphia Inquirer*. But the United States, unlike the United Kingdom or France, did not have a tradition of powerful national print news outlets. Our newspaper journalism was, like our politics, federalized.

All of that has changed in the past twenty years. Now there is indeed an unquestionably national newspaper that dominates the American journalism market: the *New York Times*. The *Washington Post* continues to have national ambitions. And even formerly foreign papers, like the *Guardian* in the United Kingdom, have tried to carve out a US national niche for themselves. The trends in the American new business seem to be toward increasing nationalization and even internationalization. And now that national news is readily found elsewhere, it's possible that citizens are less eager for the newspaper and have what seem to be reasonable substitutes—news acquired from friends, from neighbors, or even from local TV news. None of these explanations exclude any of the others, of course. And it may simply be that there is a greater diversity in business and organizational structure among news outlets with a national or global focus. But whatever the explanation, how we discuss "the future of journalism" depends a lot on what kind of journalism we are talking about—particularly whether it covers local, national, or international events.

It sounds like news coverage based on geographic location might be less important in years to come. Is that right? And if that's the case, what coverage options are there other than geographical ones?

That's probably right. News coverage of specifically geographical locations (cities, state government, etc.) will continue, but will probably decline in amount if not importance.

Despite the struggles of local news media outlets and the trend toward nationalization that we discussed in the previous question, some of the most fascinating media experiments happening today are happening locally. Billy Penn in Philadelphia is a new startup focused on young people in the city who have traditionally not found journalism to be all that appealing to them. They are doubling down on aggregating traditional news sources, conducting their own original local news reporting, and embracing a mobile-first distribution strategy. And there are other journalism outlets like the Texas Tribune (at the state level) and the New Jersey News Network (at the local level) that are pioneering exciting innovations. The Texas Tribune has a robust statehouse reporting operation, funded through a combination of live events, foundation grants, and individual donations. The NJ News Network, for its part, acts as a Montclair University-based clearinghouse for local journalism organizations to share tips and back-end resources. We are likely to see more of these kinds of experiments in the future.

But even beyond the question of local, national, or international coverage, **the future is likely to bring more and more non-location-specific news services.** Instead, we'll probably see more and more digital news arranged around the overlapping interests of small groups of people, as well as elite niches.

One thing the Internet does quite well is that it allows communities to come together around topics of shared interest, regardless of where the people who make up those communities happen to live. Imagine a small group of people with an extremely rare disease. Under previous communication regimes, these people would have been scattered all across the country or world and might not have ever come to learn there were other people out there like them. With the Internet, on the other hand, these scattered individuals can unite to share important information, and perhaps even learn enough about the illness they face that they can pool lifesaving information! And digital technologies don't just affect how we learn about rare illnesses. It affects how we learn about news and current information, too. Because news organizations (and advertisers) can now aggregate eyeballs from all over the world on particular topics, they can make a viable business out of catering to the coverage of very specific subjects that aren't bound by geographical location. And a lot of times, these communities of interest shade into elite niches—in other words, folks who share particular interests and values that might be the provenance of the elite. If you care a lot about videogames, or a particular esoteric issue in the foreign policy world, or your college rugby team, the digital news ecosystem has made it so much easier for you to have a place to go to learn about this stuff and for the organizations who provide it to make money doing so.

Beyond niche communities, even general interest news and information sites seem increasingly geographically displaced. Take Buzzfeed. What specific locality does Buzzfeed serve? English-speakers, probably. And almost certainly a swath of mostly urban-dwelling young Americans. But beyond that, Buzzfeed really isn't tied into a particular city, town, or even country in the same way news organizations of the past were. Instead, Buzzfeed embraces what we might call a "high traffic/high prestige" content strategy—posting an endless number of silly lists and quizzes, but also engaging in the collection and analysis of serious news. In other words, Buzzfeed drives a ton of its readership traffic because it produces an incredible number of whimsical quizzes, animated graphics (called graphic image files, or gifs), and lists such as "Ten Signs You Were Born in the 70s." But at the same time, Buzzfeed reports a lot of hard news, including original reporting from Washington DC, New York, Silicon Valley, and global "hot spots" around the world. This disparity—the silliness of a majority of their content combined with a niche of serious original news reporting—allows Buzzfeed to generate huge traffic numbers (good for bulk advertising) but also attract an elite audience that appeals to top brand advertisers in a different way.

In both cases, Buzzfeed is certainly not tied to a geographic locale the way a lot of news of the twentieth century was.

What about ethnic and other non-English-language media in the United States, particularly Spanish-language journalism?

The importance of Hispanic media outlets, such as Univision and Telemundo, is likely to grow in the future as the bilingual population of the United States increases. Certainly Spanish-language journalism is not the only ethnic media in the United States, but in many ways it is the most central to the daily life of an increasingly politically assertive ethnic group. As of 2013 there were fifty-four million Hispanics in the United States (17% of the total population), but most of the growth in this population since 2000 has **not** occurred as a result of immigration. As a result, Hispanic Americans are increasingly bilingual or speak English only.

How are these developments affecting the growth and health of Hispanic media in the United States? Spanish-language newspapers (*El Nuevo Herald, El Diario, La Opinion*) are not immune from the general decline of the newspaper business, with each of these three papers losing between 7% and 10% of their circulation in 2014. And while Univision's news program ratings actually declined in 2014, its total revenue grew 11%, from $2.6 billion to $2.9 billion. Rival Telemundo saw its rating increase in 2014, as well as its finances.

Hispanic media is not insulated from the general trends shaping the larger global news business. In relative terms, however, we should expect the power of these outlets to grow in the years ahead, as both the political and cultural impact of Hispanics continues to increase.

So does this mean we see news continue to fragment?

Maybe. There are two schools of thought on this.

One school of thought provides us with an unambiguous "yes" in answer to that question. What does increased news fragmentation mean, in simple terms? It means that the news outlets of the future will be forced to rely on the patronage of smaller and smaller audiences with well-defined interests and reasons for consuming this journalistic content. And this need—to forsake a mass audience and the mass advertising that came with it—will mean an increasingly fragmented world of journalistic production.

So why is this happening? Are changes in advertising driving changes in journalistic production strategies? Are we simply dealing with an empowered audience that now has more choices about what kind of media to consume than ever before? Or is technology in the driver's seat? One strategy to try to come to terms with these questions is to break down the types of causes into general "root causes." So, for instance, we might argue that technology is driving journalistic fragmentation. Or we might have evidence that changes in audience behavior are causing it. Or perhaps there are economic forces driving the changes.

Understanding the root causes of audience fragmentation is important if we are to understand the *future relationship* between mass audiences, niche audiences, and journalism. If technology is causing audiences to fragment, then we might expect that new changes in technology over the next decade or two might help news organizations "rebundle" their audience—attract readers across a wide variety of niches. Perhaps the continued growth of Facebook, for instance, will create a new "mass audience" for particular types of news. If audience preferences and economic models are driving fragmentation, on the other hand, journalists and editors might need to reconcile themselves to a world where people just consume the type of news they really care about and ignore the rest of it.

The other school of thought asks us to shift our perspective and take a bit more of a "big picture" point of view. While much about the technology of the Internet seems to be pushing toward fragmentation and dispersal, there are also globalizing trends (news articles that rapidly circulate across the globe, images of foreign protests that quickly draw massive amounts of attention, cultural preferences and consumer tastes) that perhaps draw aspects of the news audience closer together. And even technology does *more* than simply push fragmentation. While fewer people than ever might watch the news on the "big three networks" of CBS, NBC, and ABC, new digital intermediaries like Facebook and Google have become widely used mass audience platforms, even though we don't often think of them in those terms.

Perhaps the best answer to the question of fragmentation is the least satisfying. Current trends are pushing both journalistic fragmentation and the reintegration of mass media audiences. The future will see both increased fragmentation and integration at the same time.

So is this fragmentation a bad thing?

In lots of ways the answer to that question depends on your larger thoughts about how politics ought to be practiced and what your notion of the "ideal citizen" really is. A lot of future-of-news commentators speak as if digital fragmentation were universally bad. It certainly sounds terrible—fragmentation implies the shattering of something whole. But what the fragmentation of news audiences also does is that it creates new communities, and new freedoms to learn about the issues that concern them directly. Perhaps the Internet really has shattered the large community conversation that existed in the era of monopoly local newspapers and three big networks. But we shouldn't forget that that "large conversation" also reflected the narrow interests of a specific group of people and often excluded many other points of view. Now these less powerful communities can be created out of the very process of fragmentation itself, and with this can come new freedoms to engage in politics in new ways.

Will the kinds of news collaborations discussed in chapter 2 continue? How might they change in the future?

Collaborations will continue and will become more common. But they will be more likely for certain kinds of journalism than others.

Nonprofit news organizations, like ProPublica, have led the way in partnering with major newspapers like the *New York Times* and the *Washington Post*. Newspapers in Ohio are sharing content of statewide concern. Local newspapers and radio stations are collaborating with each other more frequently on items like news, TV, and, weather. It's obvious that this trend toward collaboration and sharing, as opposed to competition and "scoops," is important. But will it last?

It's important to keep in mind that collaboration is still a minority practice within the news industry. The *Washington*

Post and the *New York Times* still aggressively compete, and the papers express quiet dismay when one paper scoops the other. The *New York Post* and the *New York Daily* News act the same way when it comes to city news. Interorganizational competition is buried deeply within the DNA of most modern news organizations, and it is unlikely that these tendencies will change overnight.

But it seems clear that collaborations will become more and more important. The near-immediate accessibility of content on the Internet makes beating your competitor seem less important to the people who read the news, if not always the people who make it. The fact that so many people access news stories through web platforms like Google, Twitter, and Facebook means that they often don't even *know* the outlets responsible for producing that content. The technological ability to collaborate across institutions is obviously more possible in the twenty-first century than the twentieth. And, the relatively diminished economic standing of the traditional news business means that there will be an economic incentive to work together as well.

Certain types of collaboration will thrive while others will either diminish or never get off the ground. We can expect the most common collaborations to involve a certain type of investigative reporting, in which institutional practices of governments or corporations are exposed by a team of reporters at different news outlets. Less formal, more organic, and less frequent "collaborations" will probably occur during breaking news events, usually involving journalistic organizations linking to other organizations' news and reposting their once original content.

There are probably elements of news production that will never be collaborative—these relate to certain forms of investigative journalism, ones that involve the exposure of hidden and deceitful deeds by individuals, rather than patterns of corruption at institutions. In other words, for the foreseeable future, we should expect some collaborations to work better than others.

Facebook and news companies are increasingly working together to host some news stories. Is this another example of news industry partnership and collaboration?

It is, although some commentators have wondered how much of an equal partnership it actually is. We've already discussed the Facebook "Instant Articles" program. But the shifting relationships between Facebook and news organizations are only a single example of what some scholars and commentators have called the "platformization of news."

What they mean is this: There is a difference between functioning as a platform and functioning as a publisher. Historically, publishers were businesses responsible for creating, commissioning, financing, and publishing media content. Platforms, on the other hand, present themselves as distinctively *different* from publishers—they host content of all shapes and sizes rather than publishing content they themselves have generated. Publishers include the *New York Times*, *CBS Evening News*, the BBC, and *Time* magazine. Platforms include Facebook, Twitter, and YouTube. We might analogize platforms as being kind of like cable television—a content host and a distribution network with a lot of power.

What does all this mean for the future of journalism and news? One of the most important developments in journalism over the next decade or so will surely be the increased dependence of news organizations on platforms for traffic as well as for driving media innovation in new directions. These platforms are powerful—more powerful, perhaps, than news organizations themselves, even as they begin to act more like publishers than they did originally in making (often opaque) editorial judgments about what content to host and how. In other words, platforms no longer simply host news content that their users think is important. They are playing an active role in the business of journalism itself. "Facebook, Twitter, and YouTube are emerging as the ABC, CBS, and NBC of the 21st century—sites that attract vastly more traffic than most others," one commentator writes. Companies purely in the business of journalism will increasingly be at the mercy of these platforms—and in response, they may try to become platforms themselves.

It has been said "journalists will start having to build their own personal brands." What does this mean?

In the summer of 2013, Nate Silver—statistics wizard, inventor of the popular 538 website, and correct prognosticator of the 2008 and 2012 presidential elections—dropped the bombshell that he was leaving the *New York Times* to start his own 538 website under the corporate umbrella of ESPN. The news was particularly surprising given that, up until that point, Silver's story was that of a previously unknown but successful blogger plucked out of relative obscurity by the *Times* who went on to have a powerful impact at a major traditional news outlet. Now, suddenly, the story was being rewritten, with the *Times* losing its Monte Carlo simulation wunderkind. What exactly is going on?

One way to think about the story of Nate Silver and the 538 website is that it is indicative of a larger trend in the news business: the old, corporate brands are now less powerful than the brands of individual journalists themselves. Pioneering blogger Andrew Sullivan's decision to launch his own stand-alone website, funded entirely by donations, added further evidence to this speculation. Journalists with a strong social media presence, a unique voice or set of technical skills, and a proven ability to drive traffic were now in a newfound position of power vis-a-vis their employers. Once upon a time, a journalist depended on a corporate or institutional media brand to provide her with a voice and a megaphone for that voice. But now, digital media encourages—even mandates—that journalists be themselves and no longer hide their individuality under the cloak of an institutional voice. What's more, this trend will accelerate in the future, some commentators argue. News institutions will become a collection of powerful individual voices. "The reality is that individual brands like Sullivan and Silver now arguably have as much or more power as the traditional brands they used to align themselves with," one important Internet writer speculated. "The big question is how outlets like the *Times* and others will handle that rebalancing of power."

Future journalists will need to do more to cultivate their individual personality, voice, skill set, and presence in the larger social media ecosystem than the journalists of the mid-to-late-twentieth century. But we also shouldn't assume that, in the not-so-distant future, news institutions will simply become a collection of stars. ESPN had no problem eventually firing one of its biggest stars (the sports columnist Bill Simmons) and letting him move to HBO. Andrew Sullivan retired from blogging not all that long after he launched his own site. As for Nate Silver, the jury remains out as to whether or not his impact has been the same outside the *New York Times* brand as it was within it.

What is "entrepreneurial journalism?" Is this a Silicon Valley thing?

Entrepreneurial journalism is a term that didn't emerge until 2008 or so, but its usage has become common in the years since. Originally it was the title of a new degree program at the City University of New York (CUNY) Graduate School of Journalism. And even though the term has come to mean a number of other things since then, the original definition of entrepreneurial journalism is helpfully clear and straightforward. "Our goal," they write, "is to help create a sustainable future for quality journalism. We believe that the future will be shaped by entrepreneurs who develop new business models and innovative projects—either working on their own, with startups, or within traditional media companies." In other words, entrepreneurial journalists not only take on the traditional journalistic roles of collecting, verifying, and distributing publicly relevant information, but they have an entire second job as well. By learning about how the news business works, by being technologically savvy, by keeping an open mind and by not being wedded to the old ways of doing things, these journalists—either through starting new companies or innovating within old companies—will help chart the future of the news business itself. And along the way they might just make some money.

But isn't entrepreneurialism bad in a lot of ways? Doesn't it just accept, without protest, the fact that journalism is now a risky way to earn a living?

On the surface, the emergence of entrepreneurial journalism and the entrepreneurial journalist is a straightforward development. The journalism industry is collapsing. A lot of traditional jobs are disappearing. No one knows what comes next. "An entrepreneurial mindset" has helped turn Silicon Valley into an economic powerhouse and has revolutionized both American industry and communications. Given all this, why *shouldn't* journalists and journalism students attempt to innovate in order to push their industry in new directions?

All of this is true, but recent scholarship on entrepreneurial journalism has complicated the picture somewhat. Entrepreneurial journalism is really *three* things, not just one. It involves a sense of journalists inventing their own jobs by starting their own companies and developing new journalism techniques. It also implies a second important journalistic skill: the importance of self-promotion and personal branding (particularly on social media) to achieve professional success. Finally, entrepreneurial journalism signals a journalist's willingness to embrace work flexibly and in precarious conditions—in other words, to come to terms with the fact that the journalism industry is a tough industry, that it is unlikely to get better any time soon, and those going into it should have realistic expectations.

Once again, none of this is bad per se. It *is* important for journalists to be realistic about the business they are getting into. And there's nothing wrong with pioneering new ways to do journalism. The complication arises from the fact that most entrepreneurial journalism programs and discourses embrace a certain form of techno-market fundamentalism: the notion that the two things that will save journalism are the free market and technological developments. This discounts the possibility that the free market and technology might *fail*, and if they do, certain forms of *public* intervention might be required in order to provide the journalism that democracy requires. In other words, there's nothing wrong with entrepreneurial journalism per se, as long as it remains open to the possibility that entrepreneurialism alone might not be enough to create a positive future for the news business.

Will journalists have to know more about specific topic areas as opposed to just being generalists?

They might. It's important to keep in mind that, in general, journalists have been knowing more and more about the topics they cover for a long time. Over the course of the last century and a half, journalists have been increasingly expected to be *experts*. Subject matter knowledge on the part of reporters is part of the general professionalization process that transformed journalism from a disreputable blue-collar craft to an at least moderately respected occupation by the mid-twentieth century. Beat reporters, from early days of journalism, took pride in both their ability to understand the nuances of particular places and situations as well as their skill in translating those nuances for a popular audience.

One big question is whether the balance between types of expertise is shifting, with journalists expected to know more and more about the topics they cover. Fusion writer and editor Felix Salmon summed a good deal of the conventional wisdom on this question when he blogged in early 2015 that "there were two areas where the future remains bright [for digital journalists] . . . First for the superstars. . . . And second: old-fashioned specific expertise. Not digital expertise, about social media optimization or anything like that. But subject-matter expertise is still hard to obtain and can retain significant value, depending on what the subject is."

Is gaining subject expertise a good career move for the young journalist of the future? It probably is. In a world increasingly populated by various forms of pseudojournalism—online opinion essays, social media marketing, public relations material disguised as journalism—being an expert in a particular area is one way for reporters to distinguish themselves. And promoting subject matter expertise is good for news organizations as well. Now that media companies can target their most loyal and engaged readers, it grows increasingly important to cater to the specific and passionate interests of those readers. Thus the rise in importance of the subject matter experts. Of course, it also helps if the subject in question lends itself well to the commercial structure of the Internet, with particularly meaningful subjects including technology, economics and business, and popular culture.

That said, there will still be room for generalist reporters, especially at the startup level. However, to rise in the professional ranks, it is likely that the future will require greater subject matter expertise as a condition of newsroom employment, rather than as a consequence of it.

How else will journalism schools change in order to train these new journalists?

There have long been debates about the purpose and role of journalism school; in the early twentieth century Columbia University actually originally *turned down* Joseph Pulitzer's original bequest to establish a school in journalism there because the profession was considered "unsuitable" for a Columbia graduate. And despite the fact that journalism professionals are more educated than they have ever been, controversy about journalism schools remains. Are they doing a good job training students given all the changes to the industry in the past few decades? What is the right balance between teaching skills, teaching abstract concepts, and providing students with grounding in the liberal arts and humanities? How can schools possibility keep up with all the new technologies that are increasingly being used by newsrooms?

Despite all the debate there seems to be a growing consensus that journalism schools need to do a better job teaching their students *quantitative* (numerical) reporting skills, in part due to the explosion of digital data that defines the contemporary information landscape, in part because the skills required to adequately report the news are increasingly quantitative in nature. There is also a consensus that students are going to increasingly have to think *visually,* even if they plan on primarily being writers or working in audio journalism. This increasingly requires thinking about journalism education in terms of how it relates to other social sciences, to information visualization and design, and to the larger discipline known as "data journalism."

Tell me more about this "data journalism." Does that mean that every journalist should learn to write computer code?

There's little doubt that "data journalism" has become one of the most important subfields of journalism in the past ten years, and even less doubt that this will be a major journalistic growth area in the future. Data journalism might be defined as the application of statistical techniques to the analysis of diverse evidentiary sources such as databases, opinion surveys, and government records, and the subsequent crafting of narratives that stem from this analysis. In other words, data journalism treats data as a kind of journalistic "source," on par with other more traditional journalistic sources like documents, interviews, and direct observations. Practical applications of data journalism actually precede the emergence of the Internet, although one thing that makes today's data journalism unique is the growth of interactivity and the use of open source documents and tools.

Some of the earliest modern applications of data-driven statistical techniques to news reporting can be found in Philip Meyer's work, elaborated in the book *Precision Journalism* published by Indiana University Press in 1973. In it, Meyer urges his readers to "go beyond the anecdotal" in their practice of journalism, using coverage of the Detroit riots of 1967 as an example. Many of the journalists that attempted to explain the riots relied on traditional reporting techniques to gather their evidence, including "man on the street" interviews and interviews with protest leaders. They also began their stories by largely embracing "common sense wisdom" about why the riots occurred. Meyer, on the other hand, conducted representative surveys of city residents to accompany a series of stories about the state of Detroit in 1967. These surveys revealed that unrest was driven by what sociologists have called feelings of "relative deprivation" and a sense that while life in Detroit had actually improved in the 1960s it had not improved for everyone and had not improved quickly enough for most African Americans relative to other groups. Meyer's findings also showed that the rioters were a specific subgroup and did not reflect the overall attitudes of the area's African American residents.

Computer-Assisted Reporting (or CAR) was a new journalistic technique to emerge from Meyer's work. In the 1980s and 1990s, journalists interested in generating stories from data and using data to shed light on news developments were increasingly using computers, both to access data sets and to carry out the number crunching required to turn this information into narratives. Prominent examples of computer assisted, data-driven reporting included a 1969 *Miami Herald* analysis that used a computer to uncover patterns in the criminal justice system; a 1972 *New York Times* story that looked at discrepancies in crime rates reported by the police; and a 1988 Pulitzer Prize-winning investigation called "The Color of Money," which dealt with redlining in middle-class black neighborhoods. In 1989, Investigative Reporters and Editors founded NICAR, the National Institute for Computer-Assisted Reporting. As should be obvious from its name, CAR emphasized the technology that lay behind the data—computers—more than the original concept of precision journalism, which was more philosophical in its argument that journalists should use social scientific technique regardless of the tools needed to do it. And it should be obvious that while many data journalists are indeed computer programmers, not all are even today, and historically very few of them have been.

It's possible, however, that this is changing. Today (and increasingly so in the future) we can expect data journalism to emphasize *interactivity* (the ability of news consumers themselves to "play" with journalistic data, to personalize it, to visualize it in different ways, and so on) and transparency (making the data sets that lie at the core of data journalism open to analysis by the wider public or by other researchers and journalists). Both of these skill sets are greatly aided by a facility with software languages and computer programming.

So is the future of data journalism really just an extension of this earlier, social scientifically oriented journalism?

In some ways, yes. A number of websites—Nate Silver's 538.com, the Upshot at the *New York Times*, ProPublica, and many others—are practicing a form of data journalism that Phil Meyer and the founders of NICAR would recognize.

There's a difference, though, between *data* journalism and other computer-based forms of journalism that's worth emphasizing. There is an even newer form of quantitative journalism—we might call it computational or structured journalism—that is different from the social scientific journalism we have discussed so far. In a nutshell, this kind of journalism focuses less on the social scientific analysis of data sets and more on generating a kind of data that can be easily aggregated and processed by a computer algorithm. Rather than applying social scientific analysis to data sets, this kind of journalism tries to create a large-scale journalistic database of people, events, locations, and other newsworthy incidents that can be combined and recombined in different ways. In other words, rather than writing a five-hundred-word story on a shooting in Washington DC, structured journalism would plug the relevant information about the shooting (the neighborhood where it took place, the date, gender and race of the victim, and so forth) into a database that could later be analyzed both by computer algorithms and working journalists. In some ways, the idea of journalists constructing a database sounds ridiculous: who would want to read such a thing, and who would want to spend their day doing it? But imagine such a database about homicides in Washington DC (such a thing actually exists, by the way, called Homicide Watch) that got built over a period of months or years and might be able to eventually tell us about the politics of gun control and crime in the nation's capital. In this and a growing number of similar cases, journalists produce not only stories but, in fact, also databases designed for use by any journalists, social scientists, or other individuals who might want to make use of them. This is the promise of structured journalism, and it's likely we're going to be seeing more of it in the future.

Does that mean that the storytelling function of journalism is just going to disappear?

Almost certainly not. Indeed, one of the special things about journalism, and one thing about it that will probably distinguish it from many other data-centric ways of communicating over the coming years, is the fact that it will always be interested in telling good stories.

Even amid all the hype about data journalism, structured journalism, and computational reporting, it is remarkable the degree to which journalists maintain their fidelity to news narratives. "We use [data] tools to find and tell stories," wrote journalist and developer Anthony Debarros on his blog in 2010. "We use them like we use a telephone. The story is still the thing." In a 2011 lecture at Harvard University, Computer-Assisted Reporting pioneer Philip Meyer argued that both "narrative journalism and precision journalism are special forms requiring special skills. If we were to blend the two, what should we call it? I like the term 'evidence-based narrative.' It implies good storytelling based on verifiable evidence. Yes, that would be an esoteric specialty. But I believe that a market for it is developing. The information marketplace is moving us inexorably toward greater and greater specialization."

Even the most committed practitioners of data-oriented journalism, in short, imagine much more of a synthesis between the narrative and data-based aspects of their craft. The story-based function of news reporting appears unlikely to go away any time soon. Conveying information through narrative seems to be one of the few things that make journalism *journalism*.

But—is it true that robots will really write news stories?

Indeed. Not only will robots write news stories sometime in the distant future—they are doing it now

In 2012 news executives started paying attention to companies with names like Narrative Science and Automated Insights. Although Narrative Science began as an academic project that united computer scientists and journalists at Northwestern University, it quickly started having an impact on the real live journalism world, producing narrativized blurbs about company earning reports that appeared in newspapers like the *Financial Times*. Automated Insights, founded by a former Cisco engineer, is doing the same thing for sports stories using box scores and other sports data. And in perhaps the most earthshaking development of all, the first story about a 2014 4.7 magnitude Los Angeles earthquake was written by a robot, called Quakebot. As a writer for Salon explained it, "whenever an alert comes in from the US Geological Survey about an earthquake above a certain size threshold, Quakebot is programmed to extract the relevant data from the USGS report and plug it into a prewritten template. The story goes into the *Los Angeles Times* content management system, where it awaits review and publication by a human editor."

In essence, these companies and news organizations are using computer algorithms and simple natural-language-processing techniques to extract words and sentences from data-rich reports and turn them into fairly typical news stories. We can expect these sorts of endeavors to become more and more common over the next decade. Many commentators have even expressed concern that robots will take over the jobs of human journalists! However, what this all means for the future of journalism, news, and journalistic employment is less clear.

There are really two questions to ask when it comes to the impact of robot journalism on the future of news production. The first concerns the *kind* of stories these robots are writing. One thing that's essential to understand is that all these programs—whether they are drawing on box scores or earnings reports or earthquake information—are using a particular type of data as evidence, a type of data that easily lends itself to becoming what we might call *structured data*. As its name implies, structured data is data that comes with a built-in organizing structure, where the information within it is already in categories or internal groupings. This is the equivalent of numbers that might be found in a spreadsheet. Some journalistic raw data, like box scores, exist as structured data from the beginning, and other data, like earnings reports and information from the US Geological Survey, lend themselves very easily to structuring. And while it is likely that data processing techniques will advance rapidly over the years ahead, it seems clear that robot journalists are good at writing stories of a *particular kind*, the kind of journalism that often appears as if it was written by a robot already. In reply to those who have worried that computerized narrative journalism will replace human beings with robots, the inventor of Quakebot has wisely responded that he doesn't see programs like his and others like it as replacing journalists but rather freeing up journalists to do more important kinds of reporting.

A second question, though, is whether this type of "narrative science" makes enough economic sense for it to become a major player in journalistic production routines. The computer scientists and startup companies that produce these kinds of products ultimately rely on clients (like the *Financial Times*) to purchase their software—and news companies do not have a large amount of excess cash to be throwing around to pay for robot journalism. The actual utility of turning box scores into stories, and the cost required to pay for services to make it happen, may not make much sense for your average newspaper in 2016. These dynamics can help explain the fact that, in late 2014, the founders of Narrative Science noted they were focusing on "enterprise clientele" rather than newsrooms: "Narrative Science now courts organizations like financial-service providers who may have already invested in data-gathering services but have no idea what to do with all that information," they wrote. Financial service providers may be in far greater need of, and far more willing to pay for, the kinds of algorithmic services offered by Narrative Science than news organizations.

Are changes in the news media system feeding political polarization in American society or just exploiting it? And will political polarization grow in the future?

A 2014 Pew Research Journalism Project survey showed that people with strong conservative or liberal political views tend to favor certain news media and stay away from others. And they follow a similar pattern in their use of social media. "When it comes to getting news about politics and government, liberals and conservatives inhabit different worlds," Pew concluded. "There is little overlap in the news sources they turn to and trust."

Ideological conservatives mostly watched a single news source: Fox News. And while ideological liberals consumed a greater range of news and opinion from a wider range of sources, most of these sources were toward the moderate-liberal side of the political spectrum: the *New York Times*, the *Guardian*, the *Washington Post*, NPR, MSNBC, the Huffington Post, and so on. Liberals strongly distrusted Fox News and conservative talk radio personalities, while conservatives strongly distrusted most of the other cable and broadcast networks.

As Pew pointed out, most Americans find news from a variety of digital sources every day, but the most conservative and the most liberal news consumers have tended to engage more in political conversations and activity. And yet the academic research conducted into the relationship between media consumption and political belief paints a complex picture. Political communication scholar Markus Prior sums it up well:

> Although political attitudes of most Americans have remained fairly moderate, evidence points to some polarization among the politically involved. Proliferation of media choices lowered the share of less interested, less partisan voters and thereby made elections more partisan. But evidence for a causal link between more partisan messages and changing attitudes or behaviors is mixed

at best. Measurement problems hold back research on partisan selective exposure and its consequences.

That said, it's obvious that Fox News and websites and blogs like Daily Caller, Matt Drudge's Drudge Report, and Lucianne Goldberg's Lucianne.com are heavily skewed toward conservatives and MSNBC and websites and blogs like the Huffington Post, Think Progress, and Markos Moulitsas Daily Kos are similarly skewed toward liberals. It's most likely that the media and politicized voters are trapped in kind of a vicious circle: partisan media feed polarization in the electorate, which increases demand for partisan media, and so on. But journalism might not be the main reason why American politics have become so polarized. Changes in campaign spending laws are another reason. Demographic clustering and district gerrymanding are yet more reasons. The rise of primary elections that push candidates to appeal to their base is another. All of these macro-political factors are related to changes in journalism and the media, but not always directly.

How will the relationship between journalism and democracy change in the future?

Modern professional journalism in the United States emerged at a particular moment under particular conditions. Although journalism did not fully professionalize until the early twentieth century, the penny press marked the onset of a new kind of journalism, a new kind of economy, and a new form of mass democracy. Throughout the twentieth century as politics, economics, and technology changed , journalism changed as well, although it never strayed too far from its basic mid-nineteenth-century roots. Now, with massive shifts in other aspects of modern life, will we see the relationship between journalism and democracy change as well?

Journalism is responding to larger changes in society as much as it is driving those changes. So it's important to ask: is democracy *itself* changing in the twenty-first century? How might we expect it to change more in the future? And how will these changes affect the mechanisms citizens have used to get information about the important public events of the day? There are many possible answers to this set of questions, but let's focus on three of them. In one possible future, journalism remains much the same as it has long been, with only subtle transformations around the edges. In a second future, journalism is radically different, in part because the public and the American democratic state are different as well. Our third possible future actually takes a longer, more historical view: American democracy has *already* radically changed since the middle of the twentieth century, and journalism is actually just catching up to these changes now.

This first perspective in essence agues that, while there have been many important changes in the news business, there hasn't been a deep change in what journalism "at bottom, *is*, and *is for*." Why? Because for journalism to radically change in this way, democracy and the institutions of democracy (elections, campaign advertisements, the relationship between the three branches of government, etc.) would have to change too. And they haven't, or, at least, they haven't changed enough. In an even deeper sense, the larger spheres of society (journalism's notion of the public, the embedded understanding of democratic governance, the economic system, and so on) have not shifted enough to shift the fundamental purpose of journalistic work. Journalists still orient themselves toward a form of professional work and a notion of the public that is mostly the same as it was a century or even two centuries ago.

There is, however, a second and more radical possible future for journalism and for democracy itself. We might also envision a world in which the majority of citizens know very little about politics and care about politics even less, a world where interest groups and politically passionate actors provide not only the normative orientation for news production but also the economic means of sustaining it. In other words, journalism could come to see itself as serving many publics rather than *a* public, and could become far more comfortable embracing an agonistic system of democratic governance. In this second possible future, journalists would serve special interests rather than the polity as a whole. What's more, the very form of news work might change—it would become all about providing *intelligence* to people who have economic or partisan reasons to care about the news rather than information about the latest late-breaking general interest events. Journalism of this sort would harken back to an older, pre–penny press form of reporting. It is possible that the news of the future will be more similar to the news of the past.

The third possible future is one in which democracy is actually *stronger* today rather than weaker, as in the second answer, or largely unchanged, as in the first. In short: democracy wasn't all that strong sixty or seventy years ago, it has grown stronger recently, and the media is finally catching up in the digital age to this changed state of affairs. According to this third view, there is much greater public monitoring of government activity than ever before—more of that activity is open to public scrutiny, more of it is scrutinizable by changes in how government operates. At the same time, more private organizations are busy scrutinizing government than ever before—scrutinizing, publicizing what they find, and sometimes suing the government to enforce their view of what the law requires. The news media has not been an unchanged bystander during this growth of "monitorial democracy"; it has aided, abetted, and taken advantage of these changes. And the new digital media ecosystem—one in which a network of amateur watchdogs and professional interest groups interact with online old and new news organizations—is the partial culmination of this process.

These three answers provide us with different normative understandings of the future relationship between digital journalism and democracy. According to answer one, neither democracy nor the media have changed in fundamental and important ways. If we believe answer two, democracy has gotten weaker. And according to answer three, democracy (and journalism) are in some important ways better now than they have ever been.

Of course, we don't have to pick just one of these answers and one of these futures to the exclusion of all others. Like much else, the future is complicated. But it is not only complicated—it is also contingent. The relationship between journalism and democracy, and indeed the future of journalism in general, depends on ideas not yet considered, elections not yet held, technologies not yet developed, and accidents that have not yet happened. What is the ultimate future of news? We've done our best to sketch out some possibilities. But in the end, only time will tell.

BIBLIOGRAPHIC ESSAY

On what was likely the first newspaper, see Johannes Weber, "Strassburg, 1605: The Origins of the Newspaper in Europe," *German History* 24, no. 3 (2006), 387–412. On the colonial press in North America and the different types of early newspapers in England and its American colonies, see Charles V. Clark, *The Public Prints: The Newspaper in Anglo-American Culture, 1665–1740* (New York: Oxford University Press, 1994). A fine history of the first centuries of news and newspapers in Europe is Andrew Pettegree, *The Invention of News: How the World Came To Know about Itself* (New Haven: Yale University Press, 2014). The best and most sophisticated general history of news in the United States is Paul Starr, *The Creation of the Media: Political Origins of Modern Communications* (New York: Basic Books, 2004). The subtitle is important and accurately foretells that the book argues against views that overemphasize economic or technological determinants of the evolution of news, insisting on the key role of political contexts and political decisions in shaping the media. James Baughman, *The Republic of Mass Culture* (Baltimore: Johns Hopkins University Press, 2006) goes well beyond the study of news to include mass media as conveyances of entertainment but is a very well-informed and thoughtful account of journalism from 1941 to the twenty-first century. No work that we know of has yet done a first-rate job of incorporating the digital transformation of news into an overview and general history of news.

On journalists who are better known as writers of fiction, see Shelley Fisher Fishkin, *From Fact to Fiction: Journalism and Imaginative Writing in America* (Baltimore: Johns Hopkins University Press, 1985). Mary McCarthy's remarks on factuality and fiction are in Mary McCarthy, *The Humanist in the Bathtub* (New York: New American Library, 1964) 173–194, pp. 174–175.

On interviewing and the difference between continental European and Anglo-American journalism traditions in the nineteenth century, see Jean Chalaby, "Journalism as an Anglo-American Invention: A Comparison of the Development of French and Anglo-American Journalism, 1830s–1920s," *European Journal of Communication* 11, no. 3 (1996), 303–326; and Michael Schudson, "Question Authority: A History of the News Interview in American Journalism, 1860s–1930s," *Media, Culture & Society* 16, no. 4 (October, 1994), 565–587.

On the history of "objectivity" as a professional value in journalism, the most widely cited study (and we—objectively!—think the best) is Michael Schudson, *Discovering the News: A Social History of American Newspapers* (New York: Basic Books, 1978). A briefer and more conceptual, less historical account is Michael Schudson, "The Objectivity Norm in American Journalism," *Journalism: Theory, Criticism, Practice* 2, no. 2 (2001), 149–170. Probably the leading work of sociology on professionalism is Andrew Abbott, *The System of Professions* (Chicago: University of Chicago Press, 1988). A helpful brief definition of professionalism in journalism, and one arrived at in the context of a cross-national comparison, can be found in Daniel C. Hallin and Paolo Mancini, *Comparing Media Systems* (New York: Cambridge University Press, 2004), pp. 34–37. For international perspectives, probably the most influential article is Jean Chalaby, "Journalism as an Anglo-American Invention," *European Journal of* Communication 11, no. 3 (1996), 303–326. For the Brazilian case discussed here, see Afonso de Albuquerque and Juliana Gagliardi, "The Copy Desk and the Dilemmas of the Institutionalization of 'Modern Journalism' in Brazil," *Journalism Studies* 12, no. 1 (2011), 80–91. An excellent new collection of essays that covers both the United Kingdom and the United States is Richard R. John and Jonathan Silberstein-Loeb, eds., *Making News: The Political Economy of Journalism in Britain and America from the Glorious Revolution to the Internet* (Cambridge: Cambridge United Press, 2015).

A brief, reliable account of the history of the ethnic press is Sally M. Miller, "Distinctive Media: The European Ethnic Press in the United States," in Carl Kaestle and Janice Radway, eds., *History of the Book in America*, vol. 4, "Print In Motion," pp. 299–311. A fascinating account of the growing importance of Spanish-language news in the United States, especially on television, is America Rodriguez, *Making Latino News: Race, Language, Class* (Thousand Oaks, CA: SAGE, 1999). On the African American press, there is a good, brief overview in James P. Danky, "Reading, Writing, and Resisting: African American Print Culture," in Carl Kaestle and Janice Radway, eds., *History of the Book in America*, vol. 4, "Print In Motion," pp. 339–358. See also Patrick S. Washburn, *The African American Newspaper: Voice of Freedom* (Evanston, IL: Northwestern University Press, 2006), especially interesting on the black press in World War II and after.

The best account of the newspapers and the Spanish-American War is Robert C. Hilderbrand, *Power and the People: Executive Management of Public Opinion in Foreign Affairs, 1897–1921* (Chapel Hill: University of North Carolina Press, 1981). Lewis Gould in *The Spanish-American War and President McKinley* (Lawrence: University Press of Kansas, 1982) dismisses the role of the New York press out of hand. Mark Matthew Welter's 1970 University of Minnesota Ph.D dissertation, "Minnesota Newspapers and the Cuban Crisis, 1895–1898: Minnesota as a Test Case for the 'Yellow Journalism' Theory" traces the widespread view of press influence on the decision to go to war to post–World War I revisionist historians intent on showing (mistakenly) that British propaganda led the United States into World War I. A useful work is W. Joseph Campbell, *Yellow Journalism: Puncturing the Myths, Defining the Legacies* (Westport, CT: Praeger, 2001).

On early muckraking, Doris Kearns Goodwin offers a useful account in *The Bully Pulpit: Theodore Roosevelt, William Howard Taft, and the Golden Age of Journalism* (New York: Simon & Schuster, 2013), pp. 480–487. For investigative reporting from the 1960s on, we have cited Peter Benjaminson and David Anderson, *Investigative Reporting*. 2nd ed. (Bloomington: Indiana University Press, 1976), pp. 3–5; and David L. Protess, Fay Lomax Cook, Jack C. Doppelt et al., *The Journalism of Outrage: Investigative Reporting and Agenda Building in America* (New York: Guilford, 1991), pp. 3–12.

On new journalism, the classic reading is Tom Wolfe, "The Birth of 'The New Journalism'; Eyewitness Report by Tom Wolfe," *New York Magazine*, February 14, 1972. A fine collection of early examples of new journalism and essays about the new journalism is Ronald Weber, ed., *The Reporter as Artist: A Look at the New Journalism Controversy* (New York: Hastings House, 1974).

The most illuminating accounts of 1950s journalism are Carl Sessions Stepp, "The State of the American Newspaper: Then and Now," *American Journalism Review* (1999); and Meg Greenfield's posthumous memoir, *Washington* (New York: PublicAffairs, 1999). For data on the rise of analytical or contextual journalism, see Katherine Fink and Michael Schudson, "The Rise of Contextual Journalism, 1950s–2000s," *Journalism: Theory, Criticism, and Practice* 15, no. 1 (2014), 3–20.

On public broadcasting and the unusually low investment in it in the United States, see Rodney Benson and Matthew Powers, "Public Media and Political Independence: Lessons for the Future of Journalism from Around the World," a publication of Freepress, February 10, 2011, http://www.freepress.net/blog/11/02/10/public-media-and-political-independence-lessons-future-journalism-around-world.

A useful compilation comparing journalism education internationally is Romy Fröhlich and Christina Holtz-Bacha, eds., *Journalism Education in Europe and North America: An International Comparison* (Cresskill, NJ: Hampton, 2003).

On fraternization between reporters and politicians in the nineteenth century that today would be widely regarded as unethical, see Donald A. Ritchie, *Press Gallery: Congress and the Washington Correspondents* (Cambridge, MA: Harvard University Press, 1991); for the twentieth-century cases cited here that today journalists would almost all consider dubious at best, see Michael Schudson, "Persistence of Vision: Partisan Journalism in the Mainstream Press," in Carl Kaestle and Janice Radway, eds., *A History of the Book in America*, vol. 4, "Print in Motion" (Chapel Hill: University of North Carolina Press, 2009), pp. 140–150.

On Watergate, Woodward and Bernstein's own best-selling account is *All the President's Men* (New York: Simon & Schuster, 1974), still a riveting story—but don't miss the artfully produced film version of the same name. The reporters' much more recent assessment is Carl Bernstein and Bob Woodward, "40 Years After Watergate, Nixon Was Far Worse Than We Thought," *Washington Post*, June 8, 2012.

The story of how Walter Cronkite came to be judged the "most popular" American is told in Louis Menand, "Seeing It Now," *The New Yorker* 88, no. 20 (July 9, 2012), p. 88.

Jurgen Osterhamel, *The Transformation of the World: A Global History of the Nineteenth Century* (Princeton: Princeton University Press, 2014) is a quite extraordinarily wide-ranging 919-page history with much that touches on the edges of our subject here and ten rich pages specifically on "news."

The discussions in chapter 2 about news, journalism, news media values, ethics, credibility, and accountability were informed, in part, by three previous books: *The News About the News: American Journalism in Peril* by Leonard Downie, Jr. and Robert G. Kaiser (New York: Knopf,

2002); *The Elements of Journalism* by Bill Kovach and Tom Rosenstiel (3rd edition, New York: Three Rivers Press, 2007); and *The New Ethics of Journalism: Principles for the 21st Century*, edited by Kelly McBride and Tom Rosenstiel (Washington, DC: CQ Press, 2013). Similarly, information and analysis about the digital transformation of news and the media had roots in *The Reconstruction of American Journalism*, a report by Leonard Downie, Jr. and Michael Schudson, with research by C.W. Anderson, published by the Columbia University Graduate School of Journalism in 2009 and in slightly abridged form in the November/December 2009 print and digital editions of the Columbia Journalism Review, www.cjr.org/reconstruction/the_reconstruction_of_american.php.

As attributed in many of the section's answers, much of the research about news media change, content, and audience behavior in the digital age was drawn from various reports of the Pew Research Center's Journalism & Media Project (www.journalism.org) and The Media Insight Project of the American Press Institute and the AP-NORC Center for Public Affairs Research (www.mediainsight.org; see "Project pages" link on the site). Readers seeking reliable aggregations of current news media developments should seek out The American Press Institute's Need to Know digital newsletter (www.americanpressinstitute.org), the Pew Research Center's digital Daily Briefing of Media News (www.journalism.org/daily-briefings/), and the Poynter Institute's digital MediaWire (http://www.poynter.org/tag/mediawire/).

Data about newspaper employment of journalists and about newspaper audiences and revenue is available from the American Society of Newspaper Editors (www.asne.org/content.asp?contentid=121) and the Newspaper Association of America (www.naa.org/Trends-and-numbers.aspx), respectively. Information about staffing and digital evolution at local television stations can be found in surveys by the Radio Television Digital News Association (www.rtdna.org). The Corporation for Public Broadcasting (www.cpb.org) provides information about how news is covered and financed by public radio and television stations.

David Folkenflik of National Public Radio (http://www.npr.org/people/4459112/david-folkenflik) may be the best reporter currently covering the news media, and the *Columbia Journalism Review* provides the most breadth and depth. Insightful analysis of evolving news media economics, digital evolution, and audience involvement can be found in blog posts by Rick Edmonds of the Poynter Institute (http://about.poynter.org/about-us/our-people/rick-edmonds), Ken Doctor of Newsonomics (www.newsonomics.com), and Harvard University's Nieman Journalism Lab (http://www.niemanlab.org/author/kdoctor/). The extraordinary media commentary of the late David Carr in *The New York Times* remains worth rereading.

For the discussion of future business models in chapter 3 (perhaps the most vexed question in the entire future of journalism prediction business) we relied on the regular Pew *State of the Media* reports, which are issued yearly online at http://www.journalism.org/. We also made use of several important academic works that track the history and economics of the media business. James Hamilton, *All the News That's Fit to Sell* (Princeton, NJ: Princeton University Press, 2004) is still the most theoretically sophisticated look at the business of news. More recent work by Robert Picard has also been essential, especially *The Economics and Financing of Media Companies* (New York: Fordham University Press, 2011). The Nieman Journalism Lab at Harvard (http://www.niemanlab.org) provides regular snapshots and updates about the state of affairs for the most important media and news companies in the United States, particularly in the regular columns by Ken Doctor. Monday Note (http://www.mondaynote.com/), written by Frédéric Filloux and Jean-Louis Gassée, provides a similar service with a greater focus on Europe. For a more comparative overview of the news business we found Rasmus Kleis Nielsen, "Ten Years That Shook the Media World" (online at Reuters Institute for the Study of Journalism, Oxford, October 2012, http://reutersinstitute.politics.ox.ac.uk/sites/default/files/Nielsen%20-%20Ten%20Years%20that%20Shook%20the%20Media_0.pdf) to be essential reading.

The last decade has seen the rebirth of the ethnographic tradition in journalism research, with recent full-length scholarly books providing deep insights into the production of news, technologically driven changes to news routines, and the relationship between technology and news more generally. We drew on the insights of one of our authors, C.W. Anderson, contained in his book *Rebuilding the News: Metropolitan Journalism in the Digital Age* (Philadelphia: Temple University Press, 2012). Pablo Boczkowski's two pathbreaking ethnographies, *Digitizing the News* (Cambridge, MA: MIT Press, 2004) and *News at Work: Imitation in an Age of Information Abundance* (Chicago: Chicago University Press, 2010) remain essential reading, as does Nikki Usher's *Making News at the New York Times* (Ann Arbor: University of Michigan Press, 2014). Branching outside of newspapers, Joshua Braun's *This program is brought to you by...: Distributing television news online* (New Haven, CT:

Yale University Press, 2015) discusses technology and television news, while Lucas Graves tackles fact-checking and other emerging forms of journalistic labor in *Deciding What's True*, a PhD dissertation at Columbia University (forthcoming in 2016) forthcoming as a book from Columbia University Press.

To date, there have been few scholarly treatments of the relationship between the culture of Silicon Valley and the norms and routines of more traditional journalism. Some of the research on newsroom metrics and the evaluation of impact, particularly the dissertations and articles of Caitlin Petre and Angele Christin, come close to an analysis of this kind insofar as these audience measurement artifacts embody the general attitude of technology producers toward their users. "Innovation" as a journalistic buzzword and cultural artifact has been understudied as well, with notable exceptions, including Seth Lewis's "Journalism Innovation and Participation: An Analysis of the Knight News Challenge," *International Journalism of Communication* 5 (2011), 1623–1648, and the forthcoming dissertation research of Elizabeth Hansen, which looks at organization evolution in public radio. There has been far more work done on technologically mediated processes such as computational journalism, data journalism, interactive journalism, and robot journalism. Nikki Usher's book *Interactives in the News: Hackers, Data and Code* (University of Illinois Press, forthcoming) will be pathbreaking. The special issue of *Digital Journalism* 3(3), edited by Seth Lewis (Journalism in an Era of Big Data: Cases, Concepts, and Critiques) on data journalism is currently the most helpful resource available on technology, data, and news. C.W. Anderson's *Journalistic Cultures of Truth: Data in the Digital Age*, forthcoming, will chronicle the history of the use of data as evidence in news work.

The best books on the changing relationship between journalism and the political process, finally, primarily emerge from the political communication literature. A series of books under the imprint of Oxford University Press's Oxford Studies in Digital Politics series lead the way here, including *The MoveOn Effect: The Unexpected Transformation of American Political Advocacy*, by Dave Karpf (2012); *Taking Our Country Back: The Crafting of Networked Politics from Howard Dean to Barack Obama*, by Daniel Kreiss (2012); *The Hybrid Media System: Politics and Power*, by Andrew Chadwick (2013); and *Using Technology, Building Democracy: Digital Campaigning and the Construction of Citizenship*, by Jessica Baldwin-Philippi (2015). Other important books include Rasmus Kleis Nielsen, *Ground Wars: Personalized Communication in Political Campaigns*

(Princeton, NJ: Princeton University Press, 2012) and Rodney Benson's *Shaping Immigration News: A French-American Comparison* (Cambridge, UK: Cambridge University Press, 2013). The concept of a "monitorial democracy" is developed by Australian political historian and theorist John Keane in *The Life and Death of Democracy* (London: Simon & Schuster, 2009) and discussed further in chapter 7 of Michael Schudson, *The Rise of the Right to Know: Politics and the Culture of Transparency, 1945–1975* (Cambridge, MA: Harvard University Press, 2015).

INDEX